D1713836

BECAUSE THE WORLD IS ROUND

Because the World
Is Round

Jane Saginaw

DEEP VELLUM PUBLISHING

DALLAS, TEXAS

Deep Vellum Publishing
3000 Commerce St., Dallas, Texas 75226
deepvellum.org · @deepvellum

Deep Vellum is a 501c3 nonprofit literary arts organization
founded in 2013 with the mission to bring
the world into conversation through literature.

Support for this publication has been provided in part by grants from the Lesley
Family Foundation and the Communities Foundation of Texas.

This is a work of memoir. The events are portrayed to the best of the author's memory. Some conversations in this memoir have been recreated, and the chronology
of some events has been compressed. The names and identifying details of certain
individuals have been changed to protect their privacy.

Library of Congress Cataloging-in-Publication data available upon request.

ISBN 978-1-64605-206-6 (hardcover)
ISBN 978-1-64605-232-5 (ebook)

Cover design by Justin Childress

Illustrations by Kit Schluter

Interior design and layout by KGT

PRINTED IN THE UNITED STATES OF AMERICA

For Stephen,
the center of my world

and in loving memory of
Sol L. Saginaw and Rose Blas Saginaw

Sometimes I feel like a motherless child
A long way from my home
Freedom! Freedom!
Freedom! Freedom!

—Richie Havens
Woodstock Music Festival
August 15, 1969

CONTENTS

Preface

AS A CHILD, I ALWAYS KNEW I was lucky because my mother used a wheelchair. Whenever I wanted to, I climbed the foot pedals to her lap, rested my back onto her chest, and dangled my legs between hers. The chair's aluminum siding and padded armrests offered me comfort and security. Mom would wrap her arms around my waist in a loose hug and I was free to observe the world from our shared perspective. And when my mother rotated the wheels, I relaxed to the rhythmic clicking of her wedding band against the metal rim. I glided along with her effortlessly. I sensed the spinning wheel turning inside me, as if it were an organic part of my body. Our mother and daughter hearts beat together, trusting in the strength of the wheel that bound us. And the arrangement of those spokes held in a sturdy circle became emblematic of the way I came to experience the world: interconnected, in motion, secure.

When I began writing this book, I did not remember many specifics about my childhood. I understood that it was unusual at that time, the 1960s, to grow up with a mother who used a wheelchair because she was paralyzed by polio. I appreciated that I had a rare opportunity to travel the world with my family when I was in high school. But the impact of these experiences—and how they joined together—didn't become clear until I started to write it all down.

When my mother was in hospice care dying of cancer, I sat at her bedside in the afternoons and watched her sleep. I marveled at the life she had lived and couldn't stop pondering how she managed to do it all. How did she raise a family and pursue a career and travel the world from her wheelchair? How did she maintain her exuberant spirit? I should know! I was there! But I still couldn't grasp her fortitude and her grace. I began scribbling down small vignettes from my childhood. *Shards* I called them. I filed them away on index cards in a plastic box in my office. Memories became more vivid the more I wrote. I had two boxes. I had three boxes. I thought I might match disparate scenes together in a nonlinear way and call the remembrances *A Box of Shards*. I envisioned pieces of a mosaic for readers to combine, filling in gaps with leaps of their own imagination. But that isn't what happened.

Instead, shards began to attract each other. A scene from our travels evoked a childhood memory. Then a childhood memory called forth a scene from our travels. As the shards intersected, they took on narrative structure. The image of Mom's wheel extended beyond my own physicality, and the spinning circle became the colorful world that we explored in 1970. I recognized congruences between crisscrossing the globe as a family and experiencing the world from the perspective of my mother's lap: the comfort of family connection, the challenges of physical barriers, the appreciation of unexpected ways of living in this world.

There was nothing static about writing this book. Images from my childhood circled inside of me and connected in unexpected ways. Opportunities for interpretation grew as some memories deepened and others lost significance. I welcomed the force of these interacting recollections, and I allowed myself to follow the lead of its gravitational pull. I learned that I could construct a stable narrative with a beginning, a middle, and an end—but that the underlying stories that breathed life into the narrative turned like a wheel.

My mother died in 2009, and the interplay of memory and experience continues to this day. Now when I recall sitting in my mother's lap, I attach that experience to the times when my own children climbed onto her pedals and settled in for a ride. When I think of our travels in 1970, I am astonished by the ways in which the world has changed. Afghanistan is torn apart by war; Yugoslavia is no longer a country. And while the Americans with Disabilities Act has made life more physically accessible to people who use wheelchairs, I wonder about the experience of a child today. What is it like, sitting in the lap of a parent as their electric wheels whir up a ramp marked for wheelchair access?

Narratives end, not stories. Stories transform as memories combine with new experience and old insights get reinterpreted. Stories turn. They turn and they turn and they turn. Like a wheel. Like our world.

ONE

Dallas, Texas
September 1969

ALL I WANTED WAS TO BE somewhere else. Anywhere else would be fine. Anyplace other than where I sat now, curled up behind Mom's wheelchair in the back seat of our '67 Buick Riviera, Dad accelerating down the Dallas–Fort Worth Turnpike and through the marshland that stretched out for as far as I could see. Mom and Dad were reviewing upcoming deadlines for the sale of their automobile brake-repair shops—business, business, business. And all I wondered about was what might be happening beyond those swamps. I looked out the back window to the unobstructed horizon.

Take Woodstock, for example. Why couldn't I have gone to Woodstock? Five hundred thousand people had camped out at Max Yasgur's farm. There must have been some fifteen-year-olds among them. Richie Havens in his orange dashiki pacing that elevated platform chanting "Freedom!" like a mantra. John Sebastian sang, the warm wind blowing through his hair. The Jefferson Airplane was there. Janis Joplin. Jimi Hendricks. Imagine the experience! Woodstock Aquarian Exposition: Three Days of Peace and Music. But Mom and Dad would never have let me go, even if I had asked.

"I should have asked if I could take a Polaroid of that banker's face," Dad said to Mom, chuckling from the driver's seat. "He's the same guy, remember, who wouldn't lend us a buck five years ago when we needed it to make payroll. But now, now that we're talking about some hefty deposits—he can't do enough to chase down our business."

Mom turned her face toward Dad's. From where I sat in the back seat, it looked like her head floated above the handlebars of her folded wheelchair, disembodied. Her tight skin glowed and her smile was effervescent: "Nobody believed in us in the beginning, Sol." She lifted her chin: "It's such a great story!"

Mom and Dad were ecstatic with their success and the self-con-gratulations never ended. It had only been twelve years since they had left their families in Detroit and settled in Dallas, unemployed and weighed down by the heartache of Mom's polio. Warm weather and flat topography drew them south. Space was wide open in Texas and there weren't as many stairs. Plus the incessant sunshine meant no winter ice to push the wheelchair over. Dad clung to his upbeat salesman's attitude. *I can find a job anywhere!* And he was right. It all worked out. Look at them now—in their mid-forties and about to sell their brake-shop chain to East Coast investors for more money than they had ever dreamed of.

"So, Sol, what will we do for our *next* chapter?" Mom asked, raising her eyebrows high, her red lips glistening.

I folded my arms over my chest and examined the gray velour glued to the car's ceiling. Next chapter? I couldn't envision my par-ents doing anything new. They were infatuated with brake linings that dissipated heat, with advertising budgets for television ads, and with sales strategies to boost gross margins. As for me, I could only imagine the same old gray—coaches teaching American history at Thomas Jefferson High School, Friday night football games that I never attended, and those clean-cut boys on the team that didn't interest me in the least.

The foot pedals on Mom's chair rattled and I pressed my knee into the side of the aluminum railing trying to quiet the noise. I looked into the wheel of Mom's chair. It was like an extension of her, as personal as her stylish clothes and animated facial expressions. The metal spokes crisscrossed from the periphery of the rim to the center hub, creating X's in perfect, stable symmetry. I loved the pattern. Looking into it held my mind still, like gazing at the center of a mandala on the cover of one of my record albums.

The image of Mom's wheel is my first vivid memory. I have dim recollections of my very early years. Grandma sang me Yiddish lullabies on her screened-in back porch in Detroit. She made me Cream of Wheat in the mornings and used a wooden spoon to press an indention into the middle of the steaming bowl for the butter and milk that she added. I had birthday parties, but most of the details have escaped. There was a neighbor next door in Detroit who rode a red tricycle. There was a pet rabbit down the street. But my first real memory is of a metal circle. That sturdy wheel supported by a repeating pattern of crossed spokes.

I was two years old. The year was 1956 and my family was living in a room at the Lido Motel off Highway 67 on the outskirts of Dallas.

"*Sol—*" Mom yelled into the bathroom where Dad was taking a shower. "I can't find Janie!" Her voice was frantic. "She's disappeared!"

Mom's wedding ring clicked against the rim of her wheel as she pushed her chair between the dresser and the foot of the bed where I was hiding, balled up under a mound of blankets and sheets. I lifted the edge of my blanket and peeked out from beneath the covers. The spokes of her wheel spun toward me and stopped. The gray rubber nub was centered in front of my face, inches away. I was close enough to reach out and touch the X's of Mom's spokes and reveal myself. But I didn't.

Dad ran dripping from the bathroom with a white towel wrapped around his waist. "Harry, have you seen Jane?" he asked my brother, who was sprawled out on the second bed watching Saturday-morning cartoons. Harry was nine years old and seemed oblivious to my whereabouts. He didn't bother to answer the question.

Dad squeezed between Mom's wheelchair and my hiding place under the blankets. Water dropped onto the sheet in front of me. I stayed perfectly still, barely breathing. He jerked open the door of our room and sprinted into the motel's patio. Moments later, he returned short of breath: "She's not at the bottom of the pool."

I rolled my toes into the mattress and swallowed.

"What do we do?" Mom asked and started to weep.

I didn't know what to do either. When I first climbed under the covers, I was just looking for playful attention, like the focus of a game of hide-and-seek. My parents were always so serious, and I couldn't begin to comprehend the upheaval in their lives. I couldn't conceive of the churning instability that came with their move to Texas. I only knew I slept in a new bed and that we had a swimming pool now and ate our meals in a coffee shop. I must have felt shoved aside and deserted in the move. And now, nestled in the covers, I wanted to turn forever invisible. I felt like I couldn't move. I had caused an uproar I could never have foreseen, and my idea of play turned dramatically into a fear of being found. If I just disappeared, I could solve my problem. My parents would never have to worry about me again.

Mom turned her wheel slightly and reached for the telephone to call the front office. "We have an emergency—" she reported. "Our Janie! She's disappeared. We've searched everywhere and we can't find her."

Mom tapped the rim of her wheel's rim with her wedding ring and my attention was drawn to the pattern of crossed spokes. The familiar focus calmed my spirit. I was accustomed to holding on to that wheel as a way of drawing near to Mom. The circle was strong, and it was steady. It was sturdy support and it managed to give me courage. That wheel was a comfort; it was my mother. I took a giant breath and sprang from my hiding place, waving my hands above my head. "Here I am!" I laughed. "I'm here!"

Dad shoved his hands under my arms and lifted me from the bed into the air. He laughed and cuddled me before he kissed the top of head and set me on Mom's lap. No one said another word. I refused to leave the safety of Mom's lap for the rest of the day. I pressed into the metal structure of her corset and sank the back of my head against her chest. Mom turned her wheels and we left our motel room to sit on the patio, where we watched other kids swim.

Now, as we rambled down the Dallas–Fort Worth Turnpike in our silver Riviera, I placed my hand on the outside rim of Mom's wheel and pulled the chair toward me, still trying to silence the rattle. Dad never answered Mom's question about what they would do for their next chapter. I knew it. I knew nothing was going to change.

"You know," Mom said as she stared out the front window into the marsh. "At some point we need to ask ourselves: What is the money for?"

"I'll tell you one thing. If I ever see that banker again, I'm going to give him a little piece of my mind," Dad answered. "He's got some nerve—"

"Freedom?" Mom asked. "Does money buy us freedom?"

I filled my cheeks with air and let out a long, exaggerated exhale. Mom's probing abstractions never ceased to annoy me. Freedom. I'd never given the meaning of the word a second thought. And I'd never considered the purpose of money. Woodstock and music lyrics, that's what I thought about. Then I remembered Richie Haven in his dashiki on the six o'clock news, chanting about freedom on the stage at Woodstock. I smiled to myself and glanced at Mom's wheelchair, following the spokes to the center. Should I let go, assert myself into Mom's musing? I was comfortable tucked away in my spot, quiet and invisible in the back seat. I pressed my fingers into the soft gray nub and my smile broadened.

"We could travel somewhere," I said very quietly.

"Jane?" Mom pivoted her head around and peered over her wheelchair at me. "Honey, what did you say?"

"I don't know . . ."

"You do know, sweetheart, that when your father and I sell Brake-O, our family is going to have more money than we've ever had before. What do you think we should use it for?"

"Travel," I said with more force. "Why don't we go someplace more interesting? See the world. There is a lot more than Dallas out there." I straightened my legs and one of my sandals fell onto Mom's foot pedals. I sat up, twisting my hips and leaning my elbows onto the armrests of Mom's wheelchair. My head was positioned between my parents', and I could see straight down the turnpike. "I mean, isn't that freedom? Getting out of here?"

"Sol?" Mom asked as we continued home. "Did you hear her?"

TWO

Dallas, Texas
September 1969

MR. STEVENS SAID THAT HE HAD a challenge for me. He placed a stapled packet of mimeographed geometry problems on the upper right-hand corner of my desk and tapped it with the eraser of his pencil.

"I think these will keep you amused," he said, and when he looked at me his blue eyes dilated. Mr. Stevens was my favorite tenth-grade teacher. He was tall and painfully thin, with pasty skin and wispy blond hair. He suffered from migraines, so he missed school often, but when he was in attendance, he was one hundred percent. Mr. Stevens was concerned that I had been assigned to the wrong-level math class. He spoke to Mr. Smith, the principal of Thomas Jefferson High School, about moving me into the honors track; but nothing could be changed, Mr. Stevens was told, because I was a ninth-grade transfer to TJ, and honors classes were offered to students with high scores on their eighth-grade placement exams. I missed the opportunity for consideration because I wasn't living in Dallas for the eighth-grade testing. A pity, Mr. Smith admitted.

In 1960, after four years of living in Dallas, my family had moved to Fort Worth, where Dad opened the first Brake-O shop.

I started elementary school there and by the close of eighth grade, I was secretary-elect of McLean Junior High. My eye shadow was the perfect shade of pearly blue, my hair flipped just so, and my penny loafers clicked down the school's corridor at exactly the right tempo. I fixed an Honor Society pin to my green cardigan every Friday morning and sat in the front row of the auditorium for all-grade assemblies.

But Mom didn't take to Fort Worth the way I did. After eight years of living there, she never adjusted to the Cow Town vibe. She missed the Dallas glitz and the good friends she had made when we first moved there from Detroit. In the spring of 1968, she got the idea that since Harry had already left home for the University of Texas, and because the Brake-O business was launched, it was a perfect time to return to Dallas. She convinced Dad that Forth Worth was hampering my social opportunities. My horizon would broaden in the bigger city of Dallas, where there was a larger Jewish community. Mom never consulted me about her plan.

I circled my hair behind my ear and slid Mr. Stevens's geometry problems to the center of my desk. Intricate little puzzles—that's

how I thought about these problems. I wrestled though progres-
sions to figure out which elements solved the puzzles, measuring
angles and arcs with my protractor and building up proofs, step by
step, in my loose-leaf notebook. When I solved a problem, I felt like
I had gained insight into a little secret about how things fit together
in the world. But I couldn't solve some of the puzzles, no matter
which way I approached them. They were too complex for my
high-school theorems, and I set them aside to return to later. Mr.
Stevens said that the same geometry problems he had assigned me
had been challenging students since the time of Ancient Greece.
"When you work through tough ones like these," he said, "you're
confronting something meaningful. You're probing laws of nature.
Something much bigger than yourself."

But my world didn't feel very big. Geometry aside, my other
classes at TJ were not too inspiring—English, Spanish, American
history, and biology—mostly taught by part-time coaches and
older staff members ready for retirement. And it was hard to break
into the TJ social cliques; those friend groups had formed in elementary school and few among them were interested in the new
kids. I mostly hung out with other transfers, students like me
who'd moved in from out of town or those whose parents had
pulled them out of parochial school. I spent hours in my room
after school, door closed, spaced out on my bed, listening to
records on headphones.

One Saturday morning a few weeks after the tenth grade began, I
was back on the Dallas–Fort Worth Turnpike in our silver Riviera
with Mom. This time she drove, and I sat in the passenger seat,
fiddling with the knobs on the car's radio. Mom had a meeting at
the KTVT television station in Fort Worth, and my job was to get

her there and back. Brake-O hadn't sold yet, and she still had TV commercials she wanted to place on the air. We hadn't talked again about what the family would do with the extra money once the brake shops sold. There was no more reflection about "next chapters," just as I had expected. But the Beatles had just released *Abbey Road* and when I turned up the volume of the radio, I heard the triple harmony for the first time:

> *Because the world is round it turns me on*
> *Because the world is round—Ahhhh!!!*

I stared out the window:

> *Because the sky is blue it makes me cry*
> *Because the sky is blue—Ahhhh!!!*

It was the same Texas landscape, the identical swampland as before, but the water sparkled like glitter as the Beatles sang "Because." Ducks flew in low formation in the distance. I imagined dragonflies with fluttering iridescent wings as they managed to fly and stay in one place at the same time. Just because I couldn't see them didn't mean they weren't there. Turtles were probably sunning themselves on any dry land they could find. And tadpoles, too, darting under the water's surface, forming ripples on the top of the ponds. A whole world stirred in all that emptiness. We sped through it.

> *Ahhhhhhhh!!!*
> *Ahhhhhhhh!!!*
> *Love is old, love is new—*

"What are you thinking about, Jane?" Mom asked.

"Nothing."

"Really. You're thinking about nothing?"

"Yeah."

Mom stayed silent for a moment before she turned down the car radio.

"You can't think about nothing. Nothing isn't really a thought," Mom sucked in her cheeks. "Thoughts require words, Jane. The more words we know, the more precise we can be. The better we can share and communicate." She paused. "But nothing?" She shook her head. "There aren't words for nothing."

I turned my head farther away from her. Why couldn't she leave me alone? Wasn't it enough that I was taking her to a business meeting on Saturday morning? Didn't that satisfy her? Couldn't I just be alone with the Beatles for a while?

"Why don't you talk to me anymore, Janie?" Mom asked, and the strength of her voice weakened as she spoke.

"Experience doesn't need words."

We arrived at the television station, and I helped Mom transfer from the car to her wheelchair in the choreographed sequence of push-and-pulls we had composed over the years. She pulled herself from the car seat and propped her hip against the open driver's door. She balanced there on her right leg brace as I lowered the wheelchair from behind the driver's seat, rolling it down to the asphalt of the parking lot. I unfolded the chair and pushed it toward her, setting the brakes in place just as Mom lowed herself into the vinyl seat. Our timing was impeccable. We had perfected our silent coordination.

I steered her chair down the halls of the television station and delivered her to her appointment.

"Rose!" The KTVT sales manager hopped up from where he sat at his desk and extended a hand to shake Mom's. "Lordy, I could set my watch by your arrival," he said and quickly removed a chair from his conference table. I pushed Mom in place and set her brakes.

"Time is valuable," Mom said. "We know that." She lifted her head and smiled to one side of her mouth the way she liked to do when she felt clever and charming. She removed a clipboard and sharpened pencil from her portfolio and placed them on the table. "Well," she said. "Shall we begin?" Mom tapped her fingers on the fake-wood tabletop as if she were playing a quick piano scale.

The man looked over Mom at me still standing behind her. "Your mother is one savvy business lady," he said. "She's a legend around here." He twisted the knot on his skinny black tie and cleared his throat as he glanced down at Mom and then back up at me. "She's remarkable. But I bet you know that, don't you?"

I smiled weakly and tightened my grip on Mom's handlebars. Oh yes, I understood that my mother was an exceptional force. I heard the trope repeatedly: Your mother is brilliant. Your mother is an inspiration. Your mother is extraordinary, but you know that, don't you? Your mother this and that, spoken, always, over her head and directly to me. That was a peculiar thing about Mom's wheelchair: It separated her from people. As friendly and approachable as she made herself, people she came in contact with felt free to disregard her and talk about her in the third person as if she weren't present. Or was I just a prop? Were they really talking to Mom? It was hard to determine whether people flattered Mom by talking to me or whether they really thought that I might not appreciate the unusual woman that my mother was. I lived with her; of course I knew she was extraordinary! But I was fifteen, and I was her daughter.

"Honey," Mom looked up at me, over her shoulder. "Come back and check on me in half an hour."

Dismissed, I followed the linoleum tiling from the business offices toward the production studio. The hallway was narrow and windowless and the fluorescent lights that hung from the low ceiling created a loud echoing buzz. The walls were lined with black-and-white headshots of the station's stars: the newsmen and the weathermen and Icky Twerp, the local clown. Each man posed in the same way: one shoulder tipped to the camera, hair slicked back with pomade, a half-cocked smile. I knew those men. I had wandered the halls of this television station for years, and they had watched me grow up. At some point each one of those men had offered to help me transfer Mom from her car to the studio. When I was younger I would ask: "Excuse me, can you please help get my mother from the car? I'm Rose Saginaw's daughter." And they would reply: "Certainly, young lady, let me see if I can't be of some service here." Now that I was old enough to handle the task of delivering Mom to her meetings by myself, these men tipped their heads in recognition when they saw me.

A yellow light blinked at the end of the hallway near the upper-right corner of the studio's door. I hurried through the entrance-way before the DO NOT ENTER sign flashed red. The cool air and high ceiling of the studio was a welcome relief from the cramped business offices where I had just left Mom. My shoulders relaxed. The local weather was ready for production and the chief meteorologist, Howard McNeil, motioned for me to come over and watch the filming. I rambled over to the corner where he stood on an *X* chalked onto the concrete floor in front of an over-sized map of Texas.

"Have a seat," he said. "The show's about to begin." The weatherman grinned as he tipped his head my way and took a playful bow. I found a folding chair leaned up against the studio's sidewall and dragged it over to McNeil's stage. I lined its front legs against a strip of duct tape that marked the edge of the weather room and sank into the chair, crossed my arms at my chest.

"Stand by," the cameraman announced. He rolled the camera equipment up beside me. "The film is rolling," he said and straightened his arm out in warning.

McNeil delivered the weather forecast: thunderstorms approaching soon from the west and a high-pressure system descending.

"Cut," the cameraman interrupted. "We've lost audio connection."

McNeil pulled a red bandanna from the pocket of his pants and wiped his forehead, squinting into the spotlight. "Come on," he said. "I'm hot, man."

He winked at me.

The weatherman wore snakeskin boots with pointed tips that never showed up in the viewfinder. On TV he projected a professional look—erect posture and immaculate grooming. But something else lurked inside that man, something complex and harder for me to grasp.

"I imagine you must be in high school by now," he said. "How time flies, doesn't it?" He wiped the sweat from the back of his neck and shook his head. "I always wondered: What's your mama going to do without you if you grow up and leave home?"

I shifted in my chair and stared back at the weatherman standing on the X in bright lights. Why was he bothering me? I clenched my jaw. I'd never thought about what Mom would do when I grew up.

"Stand by," the cameraman said. "Take two. The film is rolling."

The weatherman started up again, looking dapper as usual, repeating his foreboding forecast.

Half an hour had already passed, and I returned down the hallway toward the conference room where Mom was waiting under the buzzing lights.

"Honey," she said and waved to me from a distance. "I'm over here! I'm all finished!"

The closer I got to Mom, the broader the smile stretched over her face. And the bigger her grin, the faster the blood drained from my cheeks. How would she get around if I ever left home? And how would I survive if I never ventured away? And why had I never considered these questions? I thought about the geometry questions Mr. Stevens had assigned. The ones I set aside because they were too hard to tackle. Laws of nature. Questions bigger than me. I had no way into those problems. Didn't have a clue as to where to begin.

"I negotiated one hell of a good deal," Mom said as I stepped behind her and wheeled the chair through the front door and out of the station. I turned her around and lined the back wheels up with the edge of the front steps.

"It's almost too good to be true—" she continued.

The chair bumped from stair to stair as we descended.

"Remember Marshall McLuhan? His book, *The Medium Is the Message*, about hot media and cool media? TV's hot. It's electric. All I really need is thirty seconds on TV to get my message out in a flash. And I got the sales manager to let me buy thirty-second time slots instead of the usual sixty seconds! For half price!"

The asphalt on the parking lot was covered with loose paving gravel, and I bounced Mom over it toward the car. I could have been more careful and cushioned the bumpy impact by tightening my grip on her handlebars and pushing slowly, but I didn't. I wasn't interested in Mom's physical comfort at the moment. And I didn't want to hear about her amazing media deals or McLuhan's abstract theories. The weatherman's probing had bothered me. I was shaken up and I wanted her to be disturbed as well.

"Mom?" I asked. "Have you and Dad had any more discussion about what was going to happen after Brake-O? You know, what the money is for and all that. What we might do. Or was all of that just talk?"

"Oh dear, we have been so busy."

The gravel made a crunching sound under my feet, and little pebbles flew from the side of Mom's wheelchair as I pushed her through the parking lot. I looked up at the sky. It was cloudless and clear blue and it made me want to cry.

THREE

Dallas, Texas
September 1969

MOM WAS BALANCED AT THE EDGE of her bed, naked, staring into the parquet floor of her bedroom.

"Mom? Are you okay?" I asked.

Her shoulders rounded forward, and her breasts hung toward her lap, her feet dangled, and her stomach was distended. Dad had already left for his Saturday morning racquetball game at the JCC. Usually Mom stayed in bed those mornings, reading *Commentary* or the *New Yorker*, until Dad returned a few hours later with a paper sack of bagels and smoked whitefish from the deli.

"Bye-bye, baby. I'm off," I had heard Dad call down the hall that morning, his voice as chipper as usual.

But after Dad left and I stepped from my room, Mom didn't look up when I started down the hall. She didn't call out the moment she noticed me: "Janie! Good morning! Let's talk about our day." Her eager attention usually annoyed me, but Mom's indifference to me this morning was so out of character that I was frightened.

She blinked into emptiness and spoke in a monotone. "It's the week of October first," she said. Then she looked up at me in the hallway. "That's the day I got polio."

I took a few steps and leaned my hip against the doorpost of her bedroom. When she didn't say anything else, but glanced backed down to the floor instead, I climbed into bed behind her.

The sheets were damp with a waft of Mom and Dad still lingering—faded Youth Dew and perspiration. It was common enough for me to slip into my parent's bed on the weekend, even though I was in high school. Mom needed almost an hour to dress in the mornings. Her corset took twenty minutes to strap on—aligning the metal stays, tugging and pulling and tying on the ten-pound girdle. Then there was the labor of adjusting her long-line bra, reaching behind her back, attaching the hooks and eyes. Next her fifteen-pound leg brace. And then the support hose and the orthopedic shoes. Dressing was a long and tedious process, but it opened up a nice spot of time for Mom and me to relax together. Usually Mom sat on the side of her bed facing the hallway, dressing, and I curled up behind her, facing her back. I talked, or I didn't talk, the way kids in the back of a car sometimes talk to a parent who is driving. Mom didn't need my help to dress: *Jane, hold my handlebars; Jane, steady the side of my chair*; none of that. The bed was a neutral ground and our time there was free-flowing. Mom liked to go on about something she was reading or share gossip about a friend. I listened, or daydreamed, or did both.

This morning red lipstick stained Mom's pillowcase and smeared the bottom sheet near Dad's. I balled his pillow under my head and pulled the top sheet over my shoulder as I did some calculations: October 1, 1946. Mom was twenty years old when she got polio, and that was twenty-three years ago. By now, she had been in her wheelchair longer than she had been without it. I had never seen her walk. I'd never run beside her or played a game with her on the floor, but I knew she had once been active and alluring.

I'd seen a picture of her as a nineteen-year-old girl, engaged, posing near a lake on Michigan's Upper Peninsula in a bathing suit with a boat's oar balanced against her shoulder. And I knew most of the story about how she'd gotten sick during her first year of marriage. I'd heard fragments of the tale, told in little pieces, broken shards that I'd pieced together over the years. I knew what was coming. I closed my eyes in my parents' bed that morning and prepared to hear another version of Mom's saga with polio.

"I was a newlywed," she began. "Three months pregnant with Harry when my fever shot up and my legs buckled."

Mom's wheelchair was parked beside her bed. She leaned over and pulled her corset from the nylon seat, flapping it onto her lap. With ceremony, Mom unfurled the white canvas and examined it, like she was opening a scroll and preparing to read from it. *I was a newlywed.* She always began her story that way. It sounded a lot like *Once upon a time.* And as horrible as I knew this story was, in the rhythm of those words I found some comfort. I knew I would hear about terrible days a long time ago, but I could anticipate the tale's happy ending. *Once upon a time I was a newlywed.* I rolled my knees to my chest and sighed.

My grandmother repeated life stories too. After I turned six and was old enough to fly on an airplane by myself, I spent a month each summer with Grandma in Detroit. We liked to sit on her screened back porch in the evenings, pressed into each other's arms on her corduroy couch, and wait for Lawrence Welk or Ed Sullivan on TV. Crickets chirped and her giant elm swayed as I traced the printed flowers on her housedress with my index finger and Grandma told me stories about her childhood in Vilna, in the Old Country. Gypsies told her fortune by the riverbanks near her town, and she made challah on Fridays in her one-room wooden house. It was hard for me to imagine a place like that with no cars and unpaved roads; Vilna sounded make-believe. Grandma insisted life in Europe was bitter: pogroms—murder and rape; disease—typhoid fever; starvation—potato peels picked from her neighbor's garbage. Grandma always ended her tales by saying "God bless America" and she would kiss my eyebrow while she pulled my hair from my forehead. And she always began her stories the same way: "We were five children. Orphans. Our mother died and our father was in America." Her cadence rose and fell the same way as my mother's. The rhythm to their words was a steady staccato and the substance was dramatic and foreboding. *Once upon a time we were five children, orphans, I was a newlywed, three months pregnant with Harry.* It sounded like one long continuous story.

Now Mom rested her hands on her opened corset. "We were living with my mother in a walk-up duplex on Glen Court in Detroit. My fever burned and I was too weak to get out of bed. My mother called the doctor."

My thighs tightened. I dreaded this part of the story. My mother's doctor was a Russian immigrant, too, and he was accustomed to tales of horror and woe. He dismissed my grandmother over the telephone: "You tell your daughter she's not the first girl in America to get pregnant." I imagined those two together, stuck upstairs on Glen Court, staring into each other's eyes, doomed. I didn't know which one I felt more sorry for: my helpless grandmother or my just-paralyzed mother. I just wished Mom would skip this chunk of the story and jump forward to the part about President Roosevelt and Warm Springs, Georgia, and the world-class polio rehabilitation they received there. But no.

"Your father rushed home from work on the Dexter bus," Mom continued. I pictured Dad at age twenty-four, handsome like Paul Newman, with his powder blue eyes, high forehead, and thick wavy hair. Certainly Dad knew that the summer of 1946 was a bad year for polio. October first was late in the season, but Dad must have had a sinking feeling that a nightmare was unfolding. He rushed up the stairs of the duplex and called an ambulance.

Mom removed the corset from her lap, swung it around her hips, and flattened it out on the bed. She shifted her weight from hip to hip and tucked the elastic trim beneath her buttocks. She leaned onto her left arm and twisted her right hand behind her onto the canvas, checking the stays and adjusting them slightly. Mom's body splayed onto the mattress, opening and widening, as she dropped her back between the metal supports of her corset.

"I was a charity case," she said, staring at a point on the bedroom ceiling. "They lined us up on gurneys in the isolation ward in the basement of Herman Kiefer Hospital." Mom's head was inches from my leg. I straightened my knees and rolled onto my back. Mom said there were too many patients and too few rooms because of the polio epidemic. I envisioned a dark hallway with long rows of cots crammed head to foot and side by side. She said there weren't enough doctors and that the ward attendants were afraid to touch polio patients. I stared into the ceiling along with Mom. I felt as if I was abandoned, too, helpless and unattended in a hospital basement. Why did Mom need to tell me these details? I brought my hands to my face and pulled them over my eyes. I wished I could roll off the bed and slip away.

Mom grabbed the sides of her corset, forced them over her midriff, and began fastening the hooks over her belly. Then she folded her hands on top of her stomach and rested. We both took in a deep breath. The bedroom was silent. I guessed the story had come to an end. A blue jay squawked on the patio outside the window and Mom began to slowly thread the thick cotton straps of her corset through the jagged metal teeth of the clasps.

One night, she went on, she started to weep when her legs dropped over the side of her gurney and she didn't have the strength to lift them back in place. I conjured an image of her hanging from a narrow cot facing the ceiling of the hospital basement, her pregnant belly in balance. Then my mind went blank. Enough! I couldn't listen to any more. My legs must have jerked. Mom yanked on the corset straps and cinched in her waist. Had she realized that she pushed me too deep into her gloom?

"Suddenly, out of nowhere, a little man with red hair appears at the side of my bed," Mom said, and she raised her voice an octave as if she were telling a fairy tale now.

"He says to me: 'Shah, maidelah, don't cry.' And with two arms he lifts my legs back onto my gurney. Then he says: 'It's Rosh Hashanah, maidelah. A New Year! A better year is coming!' He pushes the hair from my forehead and kisses my eyebrow. I never saw the man again." Mom threaded the cord through the eyelets at the base of her corset and tied a bow.

I only half-believed the part of Mom's story concerning the little redheaded man. *Of course* it was possible that in that dark ward, at the moment of her deepest despair, a stranger suddenly appeared and touched her with an act of kindness. It was true, I knew, that she was hospitalized during the High Holidays, and certainly the year turned out to be a better one once Harry was born, healthy, five months later. But it was also possible that the little redheaded man in the isolation ward was a figment of Mom's imagination, a hallucination brought on by the morphine she was given to control her unimaginable pain. Mom needed a hopeful end to her story. She never left her story on a downbeat. The little man provided a perfect fairy-tale turn of events: *He lifted my legs and kissed my forehead and after that magic moment, everything changed.*

That evening before dinner Dad knocked on my bedroom door. I knew it was Dad because the sound came from the top of the door, high up where Mom couldn't reach. But I could barely hear the tapping through my headphones and the loud beat of my music: John Sebastian. *Do you believe in magic?* I had stayed in my bedroom most of the afternoon, flipping magazine pages and listening to albums, trying to forget about Mom and her polio story. What could I do? It wasn't me that was paralyzed.

Dad tapped more forcefully. "Janie," he said. "Open up. Your mother and I want to talk to you."

I flung off my headphones and swung the door open without missing a beat: "It's like tryin' to tell a stranger about rock and roll!" I sang, nodding my head and looking directly at Dad.

Dad stood in the hallway and smiled. But it wasn't his normal cheerful grin. There was mysterious depth to this smile, a detached sort of amusement. He looked sheepish. His expression was contained and veiled, as if he were hiding something and wasn't sure how he felt about it. "Got a minute?" he asked.

I followed Dad to the kitchen, where Mom was sitting at the breakfast table with half a glass of scotch and soda in front of her. Dad's drink was on a coaster next to hers; little beads of condensation swelling in suspended animation. Mom and Dad shared a scotch most evenings before dinner. The doctors in Warm Springs had advised, back in the 1940s, that a daily drink was good for Mom's circulation. L'chaim! They'd clink their glasses.

I sat cautiously across the table from Mom, facing out to the street, as Dad pulled a chair up beside hers. He looked down, circling his finger around the rim of his glass.

"What is it?" I asked. "Why is everything so serious?"

"Janie," Mom began. "Your father and I have been talking about the discussion we started in the car some weeks ago. You remember. About what we might do after the business sells."

Mom paused to sip her drink and a car curved slowly down the bend of Woodford Drive. I followed the creeping movement with my eyes.

"Remember what you said about traveling? Seeing the world?"

The car crept out of sight and the street emptied. Of course I remembered the conversation. I remembered thinking that nothing would ever come of the idea.

Dad spoke: "We thought you had a pretty interesting idea there. That maybe we should take a trip together. A big trip somewhere."

My parents looked at each other, checking for clues that I couldn't see. Simultaneously, they turned their faces back in my direction.

"There's no question that you're a good student," Mom said. Her diction was practiced, as if she were delivering lines in a play. "Your report cards come home all A's. But we don't sense that you like school, Jane. You don't appear engaged."

"What are you saying?" I asked.

"We don't think that you're stimulated at your school," said Dad.

A ringing sound flooded my ears. What in the world were they thinking? Were they going to transfer me into another school? The last thing I wanted to do was to change schools again.

"School's okay," I said. "I like it! Really!"

"What if we did something entirely different? What if we talked to your principal?" Mom said. "Maybe you could take a break for a while."

"Drop out of TJ?"

"Take a hiatus," she said. "Yes."

An American and Texas flag hung side by side in the courtyard, flapping in the wind in unison. The eight o'clock bell had rung, and the halls of the school were empty when I pointed the way to the principal's office. Mom and Dad looked out of place—my father in his business suit, my mother with her shiny red lips. Nobody's parents came to TJ during school hours unless there was a big problem. My parents had never crossed inside the school's front door.

And I had never been to the principal's office. Some boys in my homeroom were called in from time to time for licks with a paddle when they got caught skipping eighth-period study hall. And I knew some girls who volunteered in the front office during lunch period, filing papers in slide-out metal drawers and taking telephone messages. I'd never talked to our principal, Mr. Smith, but I'd seen him from a distance in the lunchroom and at school assemblies, and I recognized him when he entered his office that morning.

"Mr. and Mrs. Saginaw," he said and shook my parents' hands. "What brings you to Thomas Jefferson High School this morning?"

Mr. Smith's hair was parted down the middle and slicked back away from his face. He wore browline glasses, like Malcolm X, but on him they just looked old-fashioned. Mr. Smith's office smelled musty from the textbooks that were stacked along his back wall. His desk was polished and immaculate as if he didn't have much work to do. A thin manila folder was centered in front of his armchair.

Mom rolled her wheelchair up to the principal's desk as Mr. Smith took his seat. Dad and I scooted wooden chairs up beside Mom's, and the four of us sat silently.

"So," Mom began. "I'd first like to thank you for taking the time to visit with us this morning, Mr. Smith. We know your time is valuable." Mom folded her hands in her lap, behaving as if she were making a pitch for a Brake-O ad to the TV station. "Sir," she cleared her throat, "we have an educational opportunity for our daughter, Jane, that we'd like to discuss with you." Mom told Mr. Smith about the idea that our family would like to travel next semester. Mr. Smith stared stone-faced as Mom expounded upon the positive effect that exposure to world cultures would have on the development of my intellectual curiosity. I stared into my lap. Mom was so out of touch and the idea sounded ludicrous in the context of Mr. Smith's textbook-lined office. I wondered if he had ever left Texas. I felt certain he had never heard a proposal like this one before.

"You know, sir, our daughter is an honor-roll student."

I wished I could have just gone to class. I had been enthusiastic at home when Mom and Dad and I fantasized at the kitchen table about the places we might visit—India, Istanbul, Paris. "If not now, when?" Mom had goaded me on, giddily. But there was nothing lighthearted about Mr. Smith's expression now, and I was embarrassed by Mom's sales pitch: I wasn't a commodity.

"I'm just a high school principal," Mr. Smith said and he removed his browlines to rub his eyes. "I don't make this state's laws. That's all done down in Austin." He returned his glasses to his face and his eyes looked brighter, clearer. "But if I'm not mistaken, there is no rule against withdrawing a student from high school for a semester." Mr. Smith didn't change his stern expression, but something softened in his voice. "Circumstances arise from time to time. Illness. Hospitalization. Sometimes a student withdraws, and I don't ever know the reason why. They reenroll the next semester and I never ask a question. That's not my place. Like I say, I'm just the principal here, not the lawmaker."

Mr. Smith finally smiled. I had never noticed that he had a dimple. He opened the manila folder on his desk and scanned the two pages that were stapled together inside. Mom and Dad and I didn't move, didn't even glance at each other as the principal reviewed my record. It was as if Mr. Smith had cast a spell, and we didn't want to break it.

"She'll need to make up the second semester of Texas civics. Coach Daniels teaches that in the summer," he said and looked over at me for the first time. "You're a good student. Skipping a term of high school isn't going to hurt you."

The eight-thirty bell rang. Mr. Smith scratched a note on the outside of my folder and stood to excuse himself for his weekly staff meeting. He left his office without another word of explanation. Once the door to his office shut behind him, I looked over at my parents.

"Well," Dad said, standing up and batting his eyelashes. "Looks like we need to book some airplane tickets!"

I went over and hugged Dad's waist. Mom fisted her hands into balls and squeezed her shoulders to her ears. Her smile revealed her top gums. I started to laugh. I laughed from a new place inside of me: *I was in the tenth grade in Dallas at the time. I went with my parents to the principal's office. He reviewed my record and said I could withdraw from high school. After that, nothing stayed the same.*

FOUR

Lisbon, Portugal
January 26, 1970

OUR TAXI MOVED SLOWLY DOWN THE Avenida da Liberdade toward the Hotel Tivoli and the four of us glared out the windows into an overcast day. I was wedged in the back seat between Dad and Harry. Mom was in the front with the driver, adjusting her leg brace, snapping open her purse, double-checking her papers for our hotel reservation. When the planning for this trip began, Harry wasn't going to join us, but he was able to convince Mom and Dad that leaving law school for a few months really wasn't that important, as long as he was back in Austin for exams in May. They chose to believe him and I was thrilled. Once he left for college, I didn't get to see him very often, and I missed the time we used to spend together. Even though he was seven years older, Harry always made me feel like an equal. And he was everything I wasn't.

The boulevard was lined with giant arching jacaranda that formed a gray-green canopy over the low buildings of misty Lisbon. There was a slow-moving sense to the scene, like an impressionist painting, and our hotel felt equally old-fashioned: a plush pastel-colored carpet spread out over the marble floor and a wrought iron staircase curved through the center of the lobby. Cut flowers were arranged in a vase on the sitting-room table of our two-bedroom suite and a bellboy delivered a bottle of wine as we settled into the room. Mom and Dad poured themselves a glass and fell asleep almost immediately.

"So what do you want to do?" Harry asked me.

I had never thought about what we might do.

The particulars of our trip were of great interest to Mom, however. She planned each stop with meticulous attention to detail. Wheelchair access was her top concern, and she sent a barrage of cables abroad inquiring into logistics. Mom could tell us the dimensions of the elevators in the hotels where we would be lodging; she knew the number of stairs that led to each lobby; she could describe the seating configuration of the airplanes we would board, and the age of the carriers, and the width of the center aisles.

And she had planned our itinerary with a similar intensity. For four months, from October through January, she worked with a Dallas-based travel agent plotting out our agenda. "I'll identify a contact each place we go," she said. "Someone local to give us an insider's view." She began talking to her friends, and our trip took on shape: Edith Baker and her brother, Dolphie, escaped from Bulgaria during the war and Dolphie made his way to Lisbon, where he now distributed Estée Lauder products; Ruth Jacobson's nephew from New York was the coordinator of Peace Corps volunteers in Tehran; the Rosens' daughter married a man from India who had worked at the United Nations and they moved to New Delhi a few years ago. A brake-lining manufacturer Dad knew from Tennessee did business with the largest distributor of auto parts in New Delhi; the president of the Jewish Federation of Dallas was a friend of the woman in Paris who coordinated Jewish cultural activities in France. But I hadn't paid too much attention. We were going *somewhere* and that was all that mattered.

Now, Harry took some escudos from Dad's wallet and slipped them into the pocket of his herringbone-tweed jacket. He scrawled onto a piece of hotel stationery: "Mom and Dad—Off to explore. Be back soon," and left the note propped against the flower vase in the sitting room. I slid on shoes and tied my Peter Max scarf around my head.

One step onto the Avenida da Liberdade and I stopped. Wow! A black and white sidewalk swirled about me, an undulating sweep of ancient mosaics stretching in all directions like far-flung op art, swelling and warping. One of my shoes rested on the rising arch of white tiles and the other was planted at the cusp of a black-tiled swerve. Fabulous, I thought. The man printed on the Peter Max scarf in my hair leapt through a black and white field of stars in his colorful top hat and bell-bottom pants and one of his legs stretched out, stepping into the psychedelic world before him while planets circled his head.

"Far out!" I said to Harry. "Psychedelic sidewalks!"

"I don't think so," he said. "Portugal is about as Old World as it gets."

"I guess so," I replied and tightened the knot in my scarf. I followed Harry down the sidewalk, straddling the divide, one foot in black and the other on white, trying not to step on a line. We approached a stoplight and a trolley screeched to a stop at the curb beside us. A group of old women descended, thick-waisted and heavy-jowled, dressed in black dresses that hung to their calves and with babushkas tied in their hair. I tugged at my miniskirt.

"Where should we go?" I asked Harry.

He lit a cigarette and angled his chin down the sidewalk. Harry was tall, over six feet, and I had to take long strides to keep up with him. A cat leapt from one table to another at a sidewalk café we passed. A group of soldiers was huddled around a small round table, sharing a carafe of red wine. One of the soldiers tried swatting the cat away, but the animal jumped back onto the table, sure-footed and meowing.

"Those guys are fighting a losing war in Angola," Harry said.

I wondered where Angola was.

"Africa," Harry went on without my having said a word. "Portugal is still holding on to colonies in Africa." He shook his head. "It's ludicrous, isn't it? Even the Queen of England has put that idea out to pasture."

"Yeah, really," I said, trying to display interest as I walked at the edge of a curve beside my brother. The cool and drizzly air was invigorating, and I kept up a brisk pace as I listened to Harry expound about the development of the African independence movement and the slow demise of European colonialism. But the ideas were abstract and hard to relate to. It was curious, I thought, that historians retold the past with such seemingly clear-cut insight. How did those scholars know what was in the minds of European royalty and why they made the decisions they did? How did historians even know what had really happened? There was material evidence to go by, documents and paintings and photographs, okay, but wasn't history really just retold stories? Explanations and rationalizations? Yet Harry found history fascinating and focused on ancient dates and exotic places as if he could see them right now. He carried eight-hundred-page Cambridge University history texts under the arm of his tweed jacket and read the books like romance novels. I had learned to listen to Harry talk. I knew that as long as I listened carefully, Harry would let me follow beside him.

"Look over there," Harry smiled and pointed across the street with his cigarette dangling between his fingers. "*The Graduate.*"

The movie poster hung outside the theater with chasing lights that lit it up like a Broadway marquee. The image was familiar: a woman's leg in a black silk stocking stretched across the poster in front of Dustin Hoffman, who stood in his corduroy jacket, hands stuffed into his pants pockets, staring at the pointed foot. *The Graduate* had been playing for two years in Dallas and I had passed the poster many times at the Preston Royal Shopping Center near our house. Like everyone back home, I knew the plotline: Benjamin Braddock is seduced by Mrs. Robinson, his parents' friend, before he falls madly in love and runs away with her daughter, Elaine. Everyone knew about Mrs. Robinson's affair! And I had memorized the lyrics to the Simon & Garfunkel songs: *Are you going to Scarborough Fair? Parsley, sage, rosemary, and thyme.* But I hadn't gone to the movie. Fifteen-year-olds just didn't.

"Want to see it?" Harry asked me. "They've just released it here. It's a big deal, actually. The government censors banned the film for two years because it offended their Catholic sensibilities, but they finally caved in."

"Mom and Dad would never let me," I said.

"They aren't here, Jane. Remember? They're sleeping."

A close-up of Dustin Hoffman's face filled the screen as the movie began. He gazed over the passenger seat in front of him and his focus was intensely inward. His flight to Los Angeles began a descent and Simon & Garfunkel harmonized: *Hello darkness, my old friend / I've come to talk with you again.* I relaxed into the red velvet theater chair as if I were flying beside the clean-shaven college graduate. This was fantastic! And my expectation mounted as Hoffman stood from his airplane seat and was transported on a moving sidewalk down the airport corridor to the luggage carousel where he claimed his baggage. What awaited him? I smiled. What awaited me?

Hoffman didn't look like other movie stars of the 1960s. He wasn't glamorously handsome like Robert Redford or Paul Newman. But his thick dark hair and stocky stature and the continuously baffled look in his eyes felt familiar, like he could be a friend of Harry's, a fraternity brother down in Austin. He was just the kind of boy I would like to meet and fall in love with someday: earnest and soulful, aloof and distracted by his inner thoughts. I'd never really had a boyfriend. At TJ, there were some boys I liked. Joe Moreland, for example. He had bouncy blond hair and wore John Lennon–style wire-rimmed glasses. He would guide his bicycle to his side and walk me home from school sometimes. He'd tilt his ten-speed against the front-porch wall, and we'd drop our backpacks at the door, dart into the living room while Mom napped at the back of the house. Joe played the piano and he'd bang out

Rolling Stones hits: *You can't always get what you want.* Then he'd slide from the piano bench onto the carpet, and we'd roll over the floor together, rubbing our lips raw on each other.

I didn't love Joe. I didn't long for him the way I yearned for Dustin Hoffman on this movie screen in Lisbon. By the time Mrs. Robinson appeared in her lacy black bra, I couldn't sit still in my seat. My breath was uneven and my chest heaved; my face burned and I turned lightheaded. I squeezed the muscles in my legs but couldn't stop the throbbing in my thighs. How long would this movie go on?

"It's funny," I said to Harry as we left the theater. The sun was setting and the drizzle had stopped, but the sidewalks were still very slippery. "If we were home, I'd be in Mr. Stevens's geometry class right now."

"Really," Harry said. "I'd be in con law with Charles Wright in his pin-striped suit."

"Yeah?" I looked up into the side of Harry's face but turned my attention intensely inward. "I'd be studying circles."

FIVE

En Route to New Delhi, India
February 3–4, 1970

MOM POINTED PAST A THREE-INCH plaster of paris maharaja
that balanced on the Air India counter and wagged a finger at the
attendant who was leaning against the wooden console.

"No, sir," she said. "I believe it is you that does not understand."

Dad clenched the handlebars of her wheelchair and I stood to
the side, ready to help, in the Leonardo da Vinci Airport in Rome.
It was after midnight, and we had been waiting for well over an
hour for this airline counter to open. We'd come early so that we
would be the first passengers in line. "They must see me the very
first thing, before they allow themselves to get distracted by something else," Mom explained. She needed to secure the aisle bulkhead seat in order to extend her leg brace and be able to transfer in
and out from her wheelchair.

"But, madam. I am afraid it is impossible," the attendant said.
"The bulkhead is set aside, reserved for our flight staff." He pursed
his lips and stood erect like a military man in his navy blue uniform
with brass buttons and braided-cord epaulets. "And safety concerns, of course. I know you must understand."

Dad pulled a handkerchief from the pocket of his slacks and wiped the back of his neck. Oh, of course. Safety was the first reason given whenever wheelchair access was refused. But Mom's bulkhead seating did not affect anyone's safety. And she had researched the issue thoroughly: There wasn't an emergency passage at the bulkhead, no exit door, and no bathroom. I looked down the deserted airport corridor for Harry. I should have wandered off with him when he left to find an *International Herald Tribune* for the flight. Harry knew how to make himself unavailable and avoid Mom's confrontations. He had no difficulty walking away. Not like me. I always felt compelled to stick by Mom's side like a foot soldier, as if my presence added credence to her pleas.

"Good man," Mom said and adjusted her spine, lifting herself taller. "I cannot travel to India if I cannot sit at the bulkhead. Listen carefully, please. I reserved this seat months ago with your central booking office. Special arrangements were made in America. In New York City." She removed airline tickets from the zippered side pocket of her purse and showed the agent where Seat 5A was typed onto the triplicate copies.

I stared at the maharaja doll on the counter as Mom's impasse with the agent deepened. The cartoony figure stood in pointy shoes on a magic carpet and his head was wrapped in a red and white striped turban. One arm crossed his chest and he bowed, eyes closed. The maharaja's mustache swept across his face in a black curve and covered the place where his mouth should have been. If he was our welcome to India, it seemed odd that his eyes were shut and his mouth was hidden from sight.

And now our Air India agent tightened his lips under his own mustache. He fumbled with the ticket before he placed it on the countertop and tapped it with his finger. He ignored Mom, looked decidedly over her head, and made eye contact with Dad.

"Can she walk, sir?" the agent asked my father.

Dad flushed. I curled my toes into my loafers and watched the color rise from under his collar to his hairline.

"Excuse me, sir," Mom answered. "I can talk." She squared her shoulders. "You understand, don't you, sir? I *talk*. But to answer your question: No, I cannot *walk*."

I searched the corridor again looking for Harry and noticed him sauntering in the distance without a newspaper or any apparent concern. I bit the ridge lining the inside of my cheek. *I can talk* was such a familiar refrain. I heard it often in Dallas. I even encouraged Mom to use the phrase sometimes in order to assert her authority in the face of people who would rather ignore her wheelchair arrangements. But we weren't in Dallas now and Mom's assertions sounded sadly ineffectual at this Air India counter in Rome.

I can talk.

Once a year every winter, Mom and I headed to downtown Dallas for the Neiman Marcus Last Call sale. Our excursion in February of 1969, just a year before our Air India encounter, began like so many others. I had walked into my parents' bedroom early on a Saturday morning, just as Dad approached Mom at her dressing table, where she was staring into a mirror, dabbing on the finishing touches of her lipstick. Mom snapped the tube of red gloss closed just as Dad rotated her chair toward him and leaned over her lap.

"Be sure to leave something for the other customers," he smiled and slipped a one-hundred-dollar bill under her blouse, beneath the strap of her bra. "You girls have fun downtown."

When Mom arched her back and lifted her face toward his, Dad rested his hands on her armrests and drew himself closer. They wrinkled their noses and rubbed them together. A blue jay squawked on the porch outside their bedroom, and I watched it hop as I gazed through the half-drawn curtains. A swell rose through me. My parents delighted in each other. I was lucky that way.

Wallace greeted us at the loading dock when I pushed Mom from the Neiman Marcus parking garage, across Commerce Street, toward the store.

"I thought it was about time you two came to visit me," he said, grinning and scooting his metal chair away from his security desk.

I forced Mom's chair up the steep incline of a concrete ramp and Wallace met us in front of the freight elevator. He stood attentively in his pressed khaki uniform and yanked down hard on a canvas strap that split open the scissor gate of the elevator with crashing, clanging drama.

"You know we wouldn't disappoint you, Wallace," Mom said with a lively smile. "Janie and I never miss a good sale." She crossed her hands on top of her purse and stared straight ahead. We always entered the store from the service dock because stairs blocked our access at each street entrance. But Mom never seemed to mind the back-door entry. "We polios aren't like other people," she used to tell me. "We are quick adapters." True, and maybe part of what made polios different from others was the way they accepted the attention they garnered. Mom rather liked the attentive service she received from Wallace.

Wallace unhitched the iron safety gate and I turned Mom's chair around and backed her into the freight elevator. The lift's worn wooden floor creaked. Cardboard boxes marked *FRAGILE!* and *Made in Italy* had been stacked to the ceiling on our right. I imagined wrapped porcelain dishes inside, teapots with painted songbirds and pagodas. I rubbed the back of my hand against the sequined chiffon dresses that hung on a rack to our left. Yellow. Pink. Aqua. Who wore those evening gowns anymore?

The elevator jolted to a stop and the doors screeched when Wallace heaved them apart. "All right," he said. "Ground floor." He held his hand out in a sweeping gesture as if he were a white-gloved operator in charge of a customer elevator inside the store. I liked Wallace's good spirit. I liked the freight area too, with unpacked luxuries mysteriously organized. I wished I could hold back and stay behind the scenes of the store. But I turned Mom's wheelchair toward the stockroom and said goodbye to Wallace.

—

The stockroom aisles were cramped and narrow. I had to be careful with Mom's chair, rounding corners slowly past the merchandise and mannequins. A dark-suited salesman was busy in one row, bent onto a knee, sorting boxes of shoes and marking down the prices with a red pencil. "Excuse me. Excuse me, please," Mom said to him, pointing her red fingernail into the air. The man stood up and shoved his boxes to one side making room for us to pass. "This area is actually off limits to customers," he huffed. "Well, thank you, sir," Mom replied. "We appreciate you making an exception for us this morning." I pushed ahead, winding our way to the front of the stockroom, where I tapped the rubber tips of the wheelchair's foot pedals onto the bottom of a double door. It swung open on its hinges, parting like a theater curtain.

There was Stanley Marcus! He stood in front of the ground-floor elevators in a starched white shirt and navy pin-striped suit. Like a gentleman from decades past, he had a clipped silver beard and wore a red and white polka-dot tie with a matching kerchief folded into his breast pocket. Marcus made a point to greet his customers as the elevator doors opened. "Welcome to Neiman Marcus, ladies," he'd repeat again and again, one hand relaxed to his side, the other resting atop a glass display table. When he noticed Mom and me entering the sales floor from the stockroom, he drew an arm to his chest and walked in our direction. His eyes sparkled like his pinky ring.

"Dear Rose," he said. "Welcome to the store!"

Mom extended a hand, "Good to see you, Stanley!"

The wheelchair was no impediment to Stanley Marcus. He acted as if he was preparing to kiss her hand when he bent over Mom's armrest in a slight bow. He reached out and cupped her hand between his and held it for a long moment. This man who hobnobbed with Coco Chanel and Elizabeth Arden, Salvatore Ferragamo and Yves Saint Laurent, who entertained Lady Bird Johnson and dined in the circles of European royalty, focused his undivided attention on Mom. She may as well have been a Hollywood icon and the rest of the store could have faded away. Mom was in his spotlight.

"It's always such a pleasure to see you here," Marcus said. He straightened his back and glanced fleetingly at the ceiling of the store. "You know, Rose, I'd like to figure out a way to build a discreet ramp of some sort at the front entrance here. You don't need to come in the back way like that."

Mom removed her hand from Marcus's hold and placed it back on her lap. "Oh, Stanley," she said, widening her grin. "It's really not a problem." She looked up and over her shoulder in my direction. "I have my daughter here to help."

Marcus fluttered his eyelashes at me, and I felt the color drain from my face. Mom's logic was absurd. *I don't need special arrangements; I have my daughter.* Was I her special arrangement that negated the need for other plans? Or was I a given accommodation, taken for granted, so that nobody else need be bothered? In any case, Marcus seemed to recognize my predicament. It was hard for me to look his way.

"A striking girl," Marcus said to Mom and raised his eyebrows. "Lots of natural style there. She greatly resembles Barbra Streisand, I think." He smiled at me.

I pulled at the bottom of my skirt. Stanley Marcus wasn't the first person to compare me to Barbra Streisand. Lots of people made the association. My dark hair was cut at an angle to my jaw, and I parted it on the left so that it fell into my right eye. The same cut as Streisand's. We both had prominent noses and similarly shaped deep-set blue eyes. We even shared a birthday—April 24. Yet usually when people said I looked like Barbra Streisand, I'd stiffened at the comparison. Streisand was an attention grabber, a glamorous diva who zoomed to a spotlight and let her voice soar. I sidestepped attention. I kept my head low and my mouth shut. So why did I feel flattered now, when Stanley Marcus made the observation? Why was I flattered now, unable to hide my smile? Was he flirting with me? Did he recognize some fledging presence, a flare I was beginning to develop? He certainly saw in me something more than Mom's accommodation. His interest lit a spark that burned in my cheeks.

"Thank you," I said and pushed the hair from my eyes.

"She's a good girl," Mom followed up.

"I'd keep an eye on her," Marcus said, and he winked at Mom before turning his attention to another customer.

Mom searched for a handbag while I wandered the aisles of the ground floor. Not much at Neiman Marcus really interested me. I wanted to dress like a hippie—bell-bottoms and headscarves. I liked fringed ponchos more than the jewel-colored cashmere on display. I looked over at Mom as she pushed herself away from one sale table and toward another, her elbows jutting into the air as she rotated her wheels. It wasn't often that I observed her from a distance. She had a sophisticated look in her green knit suit with the wide-open collar and that beige silk flower pinned high on her shoulder. Looking sharp was important to her. "It's essential that I remain up to date," she reminded me repeatedly when I took her shopping. "I don't want people to think I'm sick."

I walked over to her. "Find anything good?"

Shopping for purses was a challenge. Mom needed something that laid flat on her lap and wouldn't slide off her legs. Something with a short handle because long straps fell from the side of her chair and tangled in her wheels. The style of the sixties was shoulder straps and oversized hobo bags; the clutches and satchels she sought were difficult to find. But she enjoyed her stubborn search. Handbags were some the few items she could reach for and evaluate on her own. There was rare freedom in her ability to pick up the bags, rub the leather and examine the stitching, even if the search was in vain. She didn't have to try on a handbag, after all.

"Let's go up to the Zodiac Room now," Mom said as she returned a purse to the sale table. "We'll beat the lunch crowd."

I pulled Mom backward into the elevator so that she would face its door, in the same direction as the other customers. A white-gloved elevator attendant punched in the number six on a brass plate. His manner was nothing like Wallace's. He didn't make eye contact or greet us in any way. He remembered us, though; we had been in his elevator dozens of times. He maintained a hushed decorum as the other shoppers huddled in the corner of the elevator, away from us, keeping a distance from Mom's chair. Everyone stared at the numbers above the door as the lift rose in silence to the Zodiac Room.

I pushed Mom's chair onto the thick blue carpet of the sixth floor. A long line had already formed for lunch, but Mom pointed me to the maître d' at the front of the crowd.

"We can't butt in like that, Mom," I said, talking into the air over her head. "All these people are waiting their turn."

"They don't want me in line," Mom said. "Believe me, the wheelchair is a nuisance to them all. Let's talk to the maître d'."

He stood stiffly behind a wooden pedestal in his dark suit and peered deeply into the reservation book as we approached.

"Excuse me," Mom said. "We are two for lunch."

"And do we have a reservation?"

"Not this afternoon. No."

Mom waited calmly as he studied his book.

"I need an aisle seat with a removable chair," she continued. "I stay in my wheelchair and don't get out."

I stared into the carpet at the side of her wheelchair. She always insisted upon particular seating arrangements in restaurants. At the movies, she requested early admission. Special access everywhere she went: the beauty parlor, our synagogue, the neighbor's backyard patio. It was hard for me to bear when she was so demanding. But at the same time, I admired her tenacity. She was well aware that the wheelchair made most people nervous to be around and so she made it easier for them: she explained exactly how they could accommodate her needs. This maître d' for example, had a choice: he could send Mom back down into the line, where customers might trip over her foot pedals and feel uncomfortable in her presence, or he could show us to a table with a removable seat on the aisle and redouble his attention on the needs of other diners.

"Follow me," he said and ushered us through the tearoom. He slid away an aisle chair from a table for two. "Enjoy." He smiled and I couldn't tell if he was sarcastic.

Chicken consommé steamed in demitasse cups and strawberry butter melted on our popovers. "There's *always* an extra table," Mom explained, half-justifying her behavior. "It's in his interest, believe me, to get me seated quickly and out of the way." I bent my head into the oversized menu and studied my choices.

Helen Corbitt, the Neiman Marcus celebrity chef, strolled among the tables greeting customers in her apron. She rested her fingertips on the tablecloth near the blue crystals in our sugar bowl. "Mrs. Saginaw, so good to see you," she said with a charming lilt that echoed Stanley Marcus's. "I'm happy to see that you and your daughter are becoming such regulars with us. Enjoy lunch and come back soon." Mom beamed at this competent woman and complimented her on the lightness of the lobster soufflé. "Bon appétit." Corbitt smiled and moved away.

"Now that's a fine woman," Mom said. "Very professional. She knows exactly what her job is."

And I knew my job as well. Before we left the store, Mom would want me to help her shop. The requirements were exacting: Mom needed long pleated skirts that covered her leg brace and loosely fitted tops that would stretch across her double-D chest and allow her arms freedom to push the wheelchair. No slacks. No straight skirts. Nothing short. Nothing loosely woven that might snag on her equipment. All of these needs during a time when pantsuits and miniskirts were the fashion. My job was to help her select modern outfits so that she didn't look sick.

A saleswoman approached us in the Better Dresses department. She was wearing low-slung flare pants and a tight-fitting button-front blouse that pulled across her chest. She looked like a model from the cover of *Vogue* with her shoulder-length blond hair and thick black mascara. "Can I help you?" she asked as she sorted hangers and rearranged clothes on a metal rack loaded with marked-down merchandise.

"Yes, please," Mom said. "I'm looking for something with a full skirt. I need something long and pleated that covers my knees."

I was standing behind the wheelchair and watched as the woman turned our way and then looked over Mom's head, directly at me. My fists tightened on Mom's handlebars when she flipped her hair from one shoulder and asked, "What size does she wear?"

I returned her gaze but refused to answer. I bumped my knee into the back of Mom's seat, instead, nudging her to speak. *Come on, Mom, don't let her get away with that attitude. Stanley Marcus wouldn't stand for such poor customer service. Tell her that you can talk for yourself. Come on! Show her, Mom!*

"I'm a size sixteen," Mom said, decidedly.

The saleswoman batted her lashes at Mom and then looked right back up at me. I widened my eyes: *She's* your customer. I felt sorry for the woman in a way. She looked trapped, standing between the stuffed racks of clothes, not knowing which way to turn or how to get away from us. Maybe she had never been around a wheelchair before. I rolled the chair a little closer to her in a misplaced gesture of my annoyance. I didn't think she intended to be insulting. But I wasn't about to rescue her.

"And I can *talk,*" Mom continued. "I can *talk,* but I can't *walk.*"

"Can she wear pants?" the saleswoman asked me.

"No! She. Can't. Wear. Pants. My mother wears a leg brace, and she needs a long skirt."

"I'm sorry," the saleswoman said.

I'd had enough. We were never going to find what Mom needed anyway. I jerked Mom's wheelchair away from the clothes racks and pushed her to the elevator. Mom and I didn't speak as we descended to the ground floor and trailed back through the stockroom to the freight elevator. I was relieved that we couldn't see each other's faces. I knew Mom was embarrassed—more for me, probably, than for herself. And I felt bad for her. It was a complex dynamic: she had her dignity to maintain. Was it more of an affront to be overly assertive and make people around her uncomfortable or to allow herself to be overlooked and treated as if she were invisible? I just didn't want to think about the situation. The woman was stupid, that's all, inexperienced. Let's go home.

But that shopping expedition was a year ago. Now, in Rome, nobody cared whether Mom could talk. I had no desire to encourage her to assert herself here. This Air India attendant was not a department store salesman and the question at hand was not the availability of pleated skirts, or even her dignity. If this man wouldn't let her board the plane and sit at the bulkhead, we would need to turn back and our trip to India would be canceled.

"Seat 5A?"

"Yes, Seat 5A. I must sit at the bulkhead, sir."

I dropped my head and wandered away to join Harry.

Two men from the baggage department rolled a narrow chair down the airport corridor. Seatbelts dangled from the chair's sides and the sound of the metal bouncing and scraping on the floor caught my attention. I looked over at Harry and grinned: "It looks like we're getting on an airplane."

We followed the men back in the direction of the Air India counter. The sight of that empty chair on its miniature wheels was as familiar to me as the roaring sound of an airplane's engine. The chair was covered in navy blue vinyl and had a high back that was stiff like a hospital gurney. There were no arm rails or handles attached to its sides, and the width was the exact dimension of an airplane aisle. Mom hated being transported up the stairs of an airplane in those skinny insubstantial chairs. The lack of any security on the sides left her vulnerable to a fall, and she was delegated to the care of baggage carriers. As the men rattled the chair down the deserted hallway, they looked more like an emergency crew hurrying to rescue an accident victim than they did airline assistants called upon to aid a passenger.

"She was in rare form," I said to Harry as we walked. "She was more insistent than I've ever seen her. I don't think the guy from the airlines knew what to do with her."

"Yeah," Harry said, rubbing the side of his beard. "You know, not everyone thinks Mom is the center of the world."

The mustached man with the braided-cord epaulets was leaning on his counter behind the miniature maharaja. He gathered some papers together, stepped from behind his booth, and escorted the four of us out of the airport and onto the tarmac. His heels clicked with authority. The baggage attendants followed behind with the narrow chair and joined us where we huddled near the wheels of the airplane. A steep flight of aluminum stairs led from the tarmac to the opened cabin of our flight to India.

"Well, all right," Mom said and she bit the top of her lip.

She took a deep breath and handed me her purse. Harry and I stepped away as the two men approached her side and aligned the armless chair parallel to hers. Dad stood behind Mom, stabilizing her wheels, clenching his hands on her handlebars, as she crossed her forearms over her chest and dug her fingernails into her upper arms. She stared steely-eyed a few inches in front of her as each man jabbed one hand under her armpit and thrust his other beneath one of her knees. Her neck stiffened when they scooped her into the air and Dad pulled the wheelchair out from under her. Mom hung, suspended in midair. There was a slight breeze and her long skirt flapped against the tarmac.

I pressed her purse into my chest. There wasn't anything that I could do to help. If those men dropped Mom, if they stumbled in the dark or misaligned her body so that she was off balance when they settled her into the armless chair, we would just pick her up off the ground and begin again. We would start all over. We would make this work.

"Hey, Mom!" I called over to her. "We're going to India!"

The men hoisted her higher into the air before they lowered her onto the gurney chair. Mom kept her arms crossed. There was nothing else to hold on to.

"India, Mom!"

One of the men tipped the chair back onto its tiny rear wheels, circled it to the airplane, and began lugging Mom backward up the stairs. Dad remained on the tarmac with Harry and me, and the three of us watched her ascend. She was nervous. She was off balance. She was determined to get on this flight to New Delhi. I noticed the sweat dripping from Dad's sideburns as he tightened his squeeze on the handlebars of Mom's empty chair. But when I looked up at Mom's slow and wobbly ascent, I saw that she was gently lifted and being cared for. From where I stood, she looked regal.

Mom settled into seat 5A and Dad stowed her wheelchair behind the pilot's seat in the cockpit before he took his place next to her by the window. Harry strayed to the back of the plane and chatted with a flight attendant about finding an empty row where he could stretch out for the night. I took my assigned seat at the bulkhead across the aisle from Mom's and buckled my seatbelt. Sitar music was piped in over the speaker system and I loosened the Peter Max scarf in my hair. India was as far from Dallas as anyplace I could imagine. I didn't know what to expect, but I couldn't wait to get there. The airplane gained altitude and I watched the colors of the sky outside my window undulate in violet and tangerine as the sunrise and sunset traded places.

—

An airline attendant approached. She held a tray with miniature orange marigolds arranged along its border, and she offered me a warm washcloth and a drink of ice water. She wore thick black eyeliner that curled up toward her temples and a hot pink sari that exposed part of her midriff. There was elegance about her, slowness to her gestures that I had never witnessed before. I felt almost embarrassed by her gentle attention. The pilot began flight announcements in Hindi, and I smiled when I realized that I knew what he was talking about, even though I didn't understand his words. I looked across the aisle to Mom and Dad. They were sharing a scotch and soda and holding hands.

When the lights in the cabin dimmed, I switched on my reading lamp and pulled a paperback from my carry-on bag. *The Electric Kool-Aid Acid Test* by Tom Wolfe. I had picked out the book at Taylor's in Dallas and thought it was the perfect choice for our trip—the tale of a journey into the unknown. Wolfe told the story of the author Ken Kesey and his entourage, the Merry Pranksters. It was a wacked-out narrative about hippies and LSD, about parties on a Day-Glo-painted bus called Furthur, and a philosophy of interconnectedness called "intersubjectivity." Kesey and the Pranksters coined a motto: You are either on the bus, or off the bus. Perfect! This is how I thought about my family as we began our journey: Mom and Dad and Harry and I were in it together, whatever "it" turned out to be. I crossed my legs and read on.

"Jane?"

Mom's voice was a whisper and I ignored it.

"Janie—sweetheart."

I bored my index finger into the page of my book in a display of my reading concentration. Mexico? You're kidding. Kesey and the Pranksters were going to cross that bus into Mexico with all the drugs they carried onboard? No! It won't work! They can't do it!

Mom reached across the aisle and cupped her hand on my arm above the elbow. I kept my finger on the page and I turned my face toward hers. Her eyes bulged and her skin looked ashen, even in the dark. She had straightened her leg brace and extended it toward the bulkhead, angled it into the aisle. She was poised to heave herself onto her brace and stand.

"What are you doing, Mom?"

"I need to pish."

I looked over at Dad, snoring at her side.

"Oh, no. Can't you hold it?"

"No," she said. "You don't understand. I need to go."

I looked from the bulkhead up the aisle through the first-class cabin. There was a narrow door and a little step that led up to the bathroom. No way. Even if I could manage to get Mom up there—grasping the back of the seats, gripping onto my arm, swinging her braced leg—there was no way that Mom could fit through that little door. I looked back at her and the pupils of her eyes had contracted to the size of pinpoints.

How could she do this? We were heading out halfway around the world on a trip that she had planned down to every detail. She had stair counts and elevator widths and bed sizes memorized. She knew the dates we were to arrive and the names of our local contacts and the sights we would see at each of our destinations. How could she board an overnight flight and not consider access to the bathroom? And why was it that this toilet emergency suddenly became my problem to solve?

My index finger still marked my place in *The Acid Test*. I read the passage—"Intersubjectivity, as if our consciousnesses have opened up and flowed together." The Pranksters insisted that their groups shared subjective experiences: *I-am-you-and-you-are-me-and-we-are-all-together*. I shoved my bookmark between the pages and closed the book. There must be something I could do. How could I abandon Mom?

The lights were switched off in the first-class cabin. I unhitched my seatbelt and snuck up to the bathroom with my carry-on bag. When I entered the tiny cabin, I stuffed a roll of toilet paper into my bag and flushed the toilet as if I had used it. I returned to Mom and handed her the paper.

"Hold this," I said.

"What do we do?" she asked and released her leg brace.

An airsickness bag was filed into the bulkhead between flight magazines. I wiggled it free and examined it: an orange paisley design with exotic print that said Air India. The inside was coated with a thin plastic lining. If the bag could hold airsickness, it could surely hold a stream of urine. I passed the bag to Mom, and she held it for a moment without looking up. Then she turned her face toward mine and we smiled at each other until our smiles turned to giggles in a moment of recognition. What did we recognize if not our tacit intersubjectivity?

"Everybody's sleeping," I said and shrugged.

Mom forced her hips to the edge of the seat. She lifted her leg brace at the knee and moved it to the right, forming an opened V in front of her. The airsickness bag disappeared under her long, pleated skirt and she stared blankly into the bulkhead. I stood in the aisle, my back to my mother, and shielded her in the dark.

SIX

New Delhi, India
February 6, 1970

A WAIST-HIGH HEDGE LINED THE periphery of a park across the street from the Oberoi Hotel in New Delhi and created a peaceful oasis in the middle of the chaotic city. Mom and I followed Ellen Roy down the extended driveway of our hotel to a stretch of open lawn in the center of the park. Two men from Kashmir stood next to their bicycles waiting for us. The men wore Nehru-style fur hats and white baggy dhoti. Their bikes were bulging with bundles wrapped in unbleached muslin and tied together with twine.

Ellen greeted the men in soft-spoken Hindi. She had been living in India for several years now and spoke with the ease of a native speaker. Her low voice was relaxed, and she tilted her head, nodding attentively, as she listened to the men's reply. Ellen had grown up in Fort Worth, and our families were close there. Her mother played bridge with mine most Friday afternoons and her younger brother, Roger, was Harry's best friend in high school. I remembered Ellen from Texas, but I didn't really know her: she was more than ten years older than me. But I recalled when she left Fort Worth for college—"back East" to Brandeis. "Highly intelligent," Mom had said at the time. "And equally unconventional," she added, smiling with approval. Ellen worked in New York City after graduating from college and married a man who was an economist at the United Nations. When Mom learned that they were moving to his home village in Punjab, she lifted her eyebrows and observed: "Ellen likes to move against the grain!" Now Ellen and her husband had a two-year-old son, and the family had moved from Punjab to New Delhi.

Ellen sat down in the lush grass near the foot pedals of Mom's wheelchair, and I dropped down beside her and folded my legs into a half lotus. The Kashmiri men unpacked their bikes and spread out a blanket across the lawn. They kneeled before us in the serenity of the garden and began snapping open shawls that they displayed ceremoniously on the blanket. Tomato soup red with gold and green flowers. Bright yellow with light lilac paisley. Joyful colors in unexpected combinations that reminded me of the cover to *Sgt. Pepper's Lonely Hearts Club Band*! One shawl piled on top of another: dark teal and light salmon, hunter green and fuchsia, yellow-orange and indigo. What a fantastic trip! Mom reached over for a sample. One of the men jumped up and offered it to her, spreading the cloth over her lap, allowing it to billow over her wheels and drape to the ground like a magic carpet.

"He says that he brought you his very finest quality," Ellen translated for the salesman. She gathered her curly dark hair to the back of her neck and tied it into a low-slung ponytail. "He says you can't find shawls like this anywhere else." Her even-keeled voice didn't reveal any skepticism about the man's grandiose claim. "The best in all of India, he says."

Mom lifted the wool between her hands and examined the intricate stitching, studying both sides of the fabric and rolling the fabric between her thumbs and forefingers. "It is very fine work," she said. "And I recognize good handiwork," Mom said to Ellen. "My mother cross-stitches. What do you make of the quality?"

Ellen didn't respond. She split her ponytail into two parts and pulled the hair in opposite directions to tighten the hold of the rubber band. Her restraint was curious. Ellen had arranged this meeting in the park and vouched for the man's integrity, but now she seemed to have no stake in the outcome of the transaction; she didn't appear overly impressed by the merchandise nor was she cynical about the man's sales pitch. It was as if her loyalties were divided, and she was as equally vested in the merchant's sale as she was in Mom's satisfaction with the quality of the goods.

Ellen pushed the sleeve of her cardigan over her elbow and gazed out toward the street. Her sweater was heather gray, made from blended black and white mohair. I recognized its style. Ellen's mother had knitted me the same cardigan in cornflower blue and given it to me as a present to take on our trip. "I knitted the identical sweater for Ellen in India," she had told me and grinned, exposing her top gums. I stuffed the gift in the back of my closet and left it in Dallas when I packed. It was an old-fashioned schoolgirl design with round plastic buttons and knit-and-purl ribbing. Not the look I was going for. But now, on Ellen, the sweater looked soft and cozy. I imagined her wearing it in her mother-in-law's village among the other women wrapped in saris and shawls. Or did Ellen wear saris and shawls too when she was with those women? I couldn't figure her out. She had such an unusual alertness about her—her easy smile, her calm spirit. But it was hard to know what she was thinking. She kept her opinions veiled; or were they nonexistent? Had she always been so even-tempered or was that a quality that came from spending years in India, away from her family, from Texas? I wondered what it would be like to leave home behind. I pulled a blade of grass from the lawn and split it down the middle vein. I thought that I could do it too—that I could find a different culture and live a new way.

I was lost in a fantasy about moving to an Indian village, where I didn't know the language and where there was no electricity or plumbing, when I noticed a little boy. He had wedged himself into the space between Ellen and the wheel of Mom's chair. He was small, maybe six years old, and stood about as tall as Mom sitting upright in her chair. His legs were mangled and twisted into a bony knot and he leaned onto uneven wooden crutches. His back hunched and he was missing a foot. The boy stared at the spokes of Mom's chair. Then he looked at Ellen. Then me. Black kohl circled his eyes and his teeth were yellow-orange. The boy jutted a hand in front of Ellen's chest and curled his lips into a hard ridge and moaned—a groan that rose from the back of his throat and sounded as if it began in his stomach.

I clutched my ankle and looked away from him into the array of colorful shawls.

Ellen rose slowly. "I'll be right back," she said in her even voice. She touched the boy on his shoulder and said something to him in Hindi. Then they walked across the park together and she led him past the protective hedge to the street.

"Mom?"

Mom was still studying the stitching on the Kashmiri shawls and didn't answer me. I wasn't certain she had seen the boy. But she must have heard the gut-wrenching moan. I pulled another blade of grass from the dirt. Mom and I never talked about physical disability. She had a fixed story about herself: I am a well woman. I don't have polio anymore. Yes, I'm in a wheelchair, but I'm better now. That was it. The story didn't waver. And we never really discussed her disability or anyone other's. We thought we were guarding each other with our silence—as if by staying quiet, Mom avoided her identification with the pain of others, and as if her silence, in turn, guarded me from watching her suffer. But I could tell by the way her shoulders stiffened and her lips thinned that she had plenty to say. And more than anything, I understood that our asymmetry was exaggerated now. Yes, our code of silence had provided a thin layer of protection. But it wasn't working at that moment in the park. I was fifteen and threatened by that little boy's suffering. I needed to talk to my mother. But instead, I extended my silence. Mom, I understood, was too vulnerable.

"This pattern is elaborate," Mom said, running a finger over a section of embroidery. "The paisley is more like a labyrinth." She turned the fabric toward me, and I rose to my knees to inspect the stitches.

Ellen returned to us on the lawn. Her face was flushed but she maintained her deliberate demeanor as she lowered herself back down onto the grass. "That child has been mutilated by an adult to make him more sympathetic," she said. "It's a horrible fact of life here. Criminal, actually. I took him somewhere to get care, but it is a vicious cycle, you know." She wrinkled her forehead and looked directly at me. "He'll be back here in no time, begging again. The boy needs protection," she said, "but there is no such thing."

The salesman from Kashmir angled his head to the side and smiled pleasantly as he continued layering Mom's lap with shawls. Mom raised her palms to him.

"Ellen," she said, "I think I've seen enough."

Mom selected a pumpkin-colored bathrobe with brown paisley embroidery at the border. "For Sol," she said to Ellen. "I'm better in something with sleeves. I can't really wear shawls. The edges dangle and get caught in my spokes."

—

Now a second boy approached us in the park. He scooted over the lawn on a wooden dolly, poling with his arms to propel his body forward. He stopped inches from Mom's spokes and circled his eyes around the metal rim of her wheel, just as the first boy did. And just like his, this boy's legs were twisted and bent. They looked lifeless, resting to the side of his torso like a pile of broken twigs. He glared at Mom's chair and lifted a hand from his dolly, but he remained silent and did not dare touch her wheel.

Ellen fumbled through the cloth handbag resting beside her on the grass and unzipped her coin purse. She placed some rupees on the corner of the boy's platform, where other coins already formed a pile. The lines in her forehead deepened and I couldn't interpret her discomfort. Why did she give money to this boy who didn't beg, yet she refused alms to the other?

I looked up at Mom, who was adjusting her leg brace and reset her foot on the pedal of her wheelchair, astutely avoiding acknowledgment of the boy so close to her side.

"Jane," Mom said. "Please. Let's go now."

I stood and walked around the child's platform. At least the other boy moaned, I thought. At least his voice connected him to other people. This voiceless child was too hopeless to call out and his mute presence made his suffering even more pitiful. I blinked and looked away from him too.

I pushed Mom to the edge of the park where the streetlight flashed red in front of our hotel. Ellen stayed behind for a moment and caught up with us before the light changed. She stood by me as traffic sputtered down the road leaving black puffs of exhaust hanging in the air.

"Polio," she said as the three of us stared into the noise. I felt certain that she was aware of our code of silence and was determined to destroy it. Was it my pain she felt? Her voice projected directly over Mom's head. "A crippling example of the disease. Polio is epidemic in India today. And ironically, it's the result of our modern sanitary system." I felt her peer into the side of my face, but I kept my gaze forward and gripped the handles of Mom's wheelchair. Please be quiet, Ellen. Don't talk. Don't break the taboo. But she continued, explaining that exposure to feces in open ditches had once allowed children to develop natural immunity to polio. Now that city sewers were enclosed, the improved sanitary conditions weakened children's natural defenses to the disease. "It's a plague of modernization," she said. "Our children have lost their natural protection."

The light finally changed, and I pushed Mom up the hill to the Oberoi. Sunlight reflected off the hotel's large picture windows and I squinted to sharpen my vision. I didn't know children still got polio. I thought the Salk vaccine eliminated the disease. I remembered climbing the hill outside Westcliff Elementary School in the summer of 1962, when I got my polio vaccine.

It was a Saturday and I was eight years old. I sat beside Mom in the front seat of her Riviera in my shorts and red sneakers as she drove up to the sloping knoll at the side of the Westcliff Elementary School playground. It was the identical spot where she normally dropped me off for school, but on this day the place felt foreign—a long line of families snaked through the grass leading to the red-brick gymnasium. Children clung to their parents' legs. Parents cupped their hands to their hairlines, shielding themselves in the morning glare. Jitters electrified in the air.

"The school nurse is set to meet us here at nine o'clock," Mom said. "Do you see her anywhere?"

I rolled down the car window to let a breeze in as Mom shifted in her seat scanning the playground.

"It's just a sugar cube," she said nervously. "The Salk vaccine. All the medicine is inside the sugar, and you won't even notice it is there."

I peered out at the winding line of families, determined not to look at the strain on Mom's face. She didn't understand that I wasn't afraid of taking the medicine. What I feared was that she would talk about polio and tell me all those sad stories about children who got sick and became paralyzed for life. I guarded myself against those stories. Just like I shielded myself from looking at the March of Dimes poster propped up near the grocery line at our A&P. I always turned my eyes to the Tootsie Rolls and Dubble Bubble gum in order to avoid the gaze in the photograph of that crippled little girl. She posed in her party dress, leaning into crutches with braces on her legs and deep circles under her eyes, pleading for spare change to be dropped into a plastic container on behalf of children with polio.

"Children won't get polio anymore," Mom said. "Jonas Salk is making sure of that. And the March of Dimes is sending his vaccine to children everywhere. We don't have to worry anymore. We have a good medicine now."

I shifted away from her, closer to the open window, and the skin on my legs stuck to the car's vinyl seat. Mom reached over and cupped her hand on my leg. Of course she thought she was protecting me by talking about the end of polio epidemics, but the more she spoke of the disease, the more disturbed I became. Just don't talk about it, Mom. Don't tell me about how you got sick as a newlywed in Detroit. And don't start to cry. Please don't cry! My greatest fear was that Mom would talk about polio and she would begin to weep and I would be stuck—listening, absorbing, helpless. Even then, I knew that it was best for us to just stay quiet.

Nurse Brown approached our car, breathless from rushing through the schoolyard. She was in her white uniform and tie-up shoes, and she shoved her clipboard under her arm as she leaned into our window.

"Good morning, ladies," she said. "We are all set and ready to go."

She handed the clipboard to Mom, who signed the medical release. Then she opened our car door and extended her hand to me. I walked with her up the mound, bypassing the line of nervous families, and we entered the gym, where long folding tables had been assembled on the basketball court. Miniature Dixie cups were lined up in rows on the tables, each with a sugar cube set in the center. I sat at a wooden school desk and the nurse handed me a cup and smiled.

"Just let it dissolve," she said.

I tossed my head back without hesitation and the sugar cube tumbled to the back of my throat.

"You certainly are a brave young girl," Nurse Brown said. I must have appeared stoic, dutifully following her instructions to swallow the vaccine. I didn't feel brave, though. What was courageous about following instructions and doing what was expected of me? But I did think about the phone calls that Mom must have made to arrange for my special reception by the nurse. I could hear her imploring: "Nurse Brown, certainly no one understands the importance of the polio vaccine more than I do. I am, in fact, a survivor of the disease. I am in a wheelchair now and I can't manage the stairs to your school. I need your help, please—"

"Your mother, too," the nurse said, and her smile tightened. "You should be proud of her. She's a very strong woman."

The sugar melted into liquid at the back of my throat. I didn't know live poliovirus was in the vaccine, and I certainly didn't understand that there was a chance I could contract polio from the exposure. I just closed my eyes and enjoyed the sweet taste as poliovirus seeped into my bloodstream.

Dad was waiting for us in the lobby of the Oberoi when Mom and I entered through the imposing glass doors with Ellen. He leaned over to kiss Mom and noticed the Kashmir embroidery folded on her lap.

"What did you find that you couldn't live without?" he chuckled as he straightened his back.

We pulled up chairs around an oversized coffee table overlooking the hotel's garden and ordered Cokes and homemade potato chips from a man in a white silk turban. Mom handed Dad his present.

"Just what I've always wanted," he said with an equal amount of sarcasm and good nature. "A wool bathrobe—"

"But Dad," I said. "You would have loved our salesman. He was a pro. We couldn't resist. *You can't get this bathrobe anywhere else in India!*"

I told Dad about the zany color combinations of the shawls and Mom described the gallantry of the salesman's display in the park. We laughed about the boastful claims made, but neither of us mentioned the deformed children we encountered. We didn't tell Dad about India's polio epidemic, that curse of modernization. Nor did we mention the pleading sound of the begging boy or the devastating silence of the crippled child with polio.

The three of us laughed in the lobby while Ellen buttoned up the front of her mohair sweater and sipped her Coca-Cola. She leaned back into the cushion of her chair; her eyes remained calm but she curled up her lips and as she watched us carry on. Only then did I imagine what she must have been thinking: Do they know where they are?

En Route to Agra, India
February 8, 1970

"Do you see what I see?" Mom asked.

I was in the back seat of our touring car between Mom and Harry, and Dad was in the front with our driver from New Delhi. Ellen had arranged for us to see the sights of the Golden Triangle —the two-day New Delhi–Jaipur–Agra tourist circuit. It was midafternoon and we had just finished a lavish lunch in the pink city of Jaipur and were heading east to Agra for the night. The next morning, we would watch the sun rise over the Taj Mahal.

"Dancing bears!" Mom shouted out.

I twisted around to look past Harry, across the road. Two brown bears had reared up on their hind legs, shoved their paws onto each other's shoulders, and were wobbling in a circle. I would never have described them as dancing. Stumbling maybe. Struggling seemed more apt. The bears lumbered, stiff and awkward on their stubby back legs, and I could see the heavy chains weighing down their ankles.

"Sol," Mom went on, "we have to get a picture of this! See if the driver can pull over for a moment."

Dad swung his arm over the back of his seat and looked at us quizzically. I shook my head. No. Let's keep going. Those bears looked like a pathetic tourist trap. Anyway, Ellen had given us a strict warning when she sent us off on the road that morning: do *not* stop the car along the way. She assured us that our driver was an excellent escort, a responsible and dignified man, but that he didn't speak English and was only authorized to stop in Jaipur and Agra. "He knows the route well," she said. "I hire him myself from time to time." She spoke to him in Hindi and then repeated to us: "He knows exactly where to stop." She smiled: "The rural folks aren't always hospitable to foreigners."

Dad tapped our driver on the arm, but the man ignored him and kept his attention focused on the road. So Dad chuckled a bit to get his attention and pointed over to the bears as Mom handed Dad our camera.

"We want to take some photographs," Dad said loudly, as if more volume to his voice would make his words understandable.

The driver glanced at Dad briefly and returned to his job.

"Stop. Please," Dad said and waved his camera at the side of the driver's face.

Slowly, our car shifted gears and we drifted to the shoulder of the road to Agra.

Mom rolled down her window and propped an elbow on the sill, watching Dad, Harry, and me leave the car and cross over to where the bears performed. Two men tended the animals and as we approached, they tugged on the collars and the bears reared taller, grunting in their muzzles, turning pitiful turns. Spittle gathered at the corner of their mouths and dripped from their pointed teeth. I could smell the rancid breath of those trapped captives.

Dad snapped some pictures. "It's crazy, isn't it?" he said. "Here we are." Dad raised his palms to the sky and looked up. "Nobody knows where the hell we are." The bears shuffled and Dad took another shot. "But there are bears dancing on the side of the road. It's the middle of nowhere!"

Dad thanked the bear-handlers for their show and gave them some rupees from his pocket. I avoided eye contact with the men. To Mom and Dad, this exotic display of control might be entertaining, but I found it cruel that the animals were chained and made to perform. It bothered me that these bears had been captured and removed from their homes. Anyway, bears don't dance. Bears roam. And bears attack. They can bite.

I stepped away from the men and headed toward the car, while Harry and Dad lingered outside in the great expanse and lit cigarettes.

"Let's go," Mom shouted to them from across the street. "No more delays. It's getting late."

The sky dimmed over the countryside and the horizon blurred as smoke rose in columns from the villages along the roadside.

"It's mealtime," Mom said. "Kitchen smoke creates all this haze. Everything darkens at mealtime. Can you smell it?"

"Cow dung," Dad replied. "It smells like shit," he said. "But they are so smart around here. So industrious. Nothing is wasted. Cow dung for fuel, why the hell not? We can learn a lot from these people. Everything has value. Everything."

I thought the burning smell had a calming, earthy tinge. I liked the way the smoke turned the sky hazy gray-purple. And I liked the gentle pace to life outside our window. Men sauntered along the side of the road kicking up dust with their bare feet, sickles swaying from the waists of their lungis. Oxen plowed through mud and buffalo lumbered in the far-off fields, while children played in clusters by the side of their houses. Now and then a car approached ours, traveling in the opposite direction, and in this unobtrusive land-scape the sound of a passing vehicle made a whooshing sound like a rocket flying past us in slow motion.

I kept thinking about the dancing bears. When Mom asked: *Do you see what I see?* I could have easily answered: *Not really.* We saw the same two animals, yes—but what she thought was dancing, I saw as captivity. It was like the question that vexed me as a child: You and I look at the same flower and you say "red" and I call it "red," but how do we know that we experience the same hue? A word doesn't equate to experience, does it? Do our shadows fall in the identical way? Does the wind sound the same to me and to you?

Then my mind turned to the women in the villages. Where were they? Were all of them inside, preparing food for their families? I wanted to stand among them in a colorful sari, my midriff revealed, then kneel in a circle and slap chapati onto the sides of an earthen oven, singing softly, children laughing outside, just beyond our sight . . .

CLOP—

I felt the jolt and I heard the thud and my daydream vanished. Did we blow a tire?

"Sol!" Mom cried.

Dad stretched his neck to peer over the elongated hood of our roadster as our driver shifted gears once again and slowed us to a creep. We veered off the road and onto the edge of a flat field. Some men lingered in the far distance, planting seeds or reaping crops or somehow tending to the land. There wasn't another car in sight. It was perfectly still where we were, in the middle of nowhere.

"Sol?"

I glanced at Harry, who didn't look back at me.

"Dad," I said, surprised that my voice was so tight.

"Keep calm," Dad said. "Stay quiet, please."

Our driver cracked his door open, and the squeaking sound was jarring in the silent countryside. He slipped from his seat, utterly composed, and with neither a word, nor a gesture, nor the slightest attempt to explain anything, he walked away from the car. Dignified, his head erect and his shoulders low, he abandoned us in this vast and vacant territory.

Mom reached for my hand.

"Just stay calm," Dad repeated as he turned around to face us in the back seat. His mouth made a sticky sound when he tried to wet his lips. "I'm afraid we might have hit a child."

At first, only four or five men crept from the fields and gathered by the side of our car. They huddled a few feet away from where we were parked and stared at us through our closed windows. Their expressions were puzzled, as if they had never seen a family like ours. Where did we come from? Where were we going? Soon there were a dozen or so men crowded into a semicircle beside us, talking among themselves and occasionally glancing our way. One started to yell. Others raised their sickles in the air. Were there twenty men now? More? The man whose holler rose above the rest, walked up to our car and banged his hand on the hood.

"We're sitting ducks," Dad said. "I don't know where our driver went."

The crowd quieted when Dad got out of the car. I saw the sickles go down, but I thought I also saw more men than before.

"Harry," Mom whispered, "go with your father."

Harry circled the car and stood next to Dad as Mom pressed her thumb hard into the center of my palm.

"My wheelchair's in the trunk," she said.

I pulled my hand away and wedged my fingers between her knee and the steel hinge of her brace. What was she thinking? There was nowhere for us to go. Or was Mom worried that a stranger might lift her wheelchair from the trunk and keep us imprisoned in the car? I didn't know what was on her mind or why she focused on the location of her wheelchair. I didn't know what was happening here. What was I supposed to do? Did our driver hit a child?

"Don't worry," I said to Mom. "Our trunk's locked."

Was there a child on the side of the road? I don't think I saw one. Or did I? Did I see, from the side of my eye, two children playing?

I focused out the window. Dad and Harry had angled their backs toward the car's hood and faced out to the crowd of men. Dad gestured to the patch pocket of Harry's denim work shirt and Harry took out a pack of Dunhills. Harry liked to pick up the fancy British cigarettes when we passed through airport duty-free shops. He thought the gold rim and sleek red box had a sophisticated James Bond look. Maybe so. But out here on this dusty Indian roadside, that shiny gilded box with the elaborate crest of Her Majesty on the front looked ludicrous.

Dad reached for the cigarette box and held it ceremoniously, inches in front of his chest. The men stepped cautiously toward him, craning to get a better view of the carton's elegance. Slowly, Dad slid open the top and revealed a neat double row of perfectly lined-up smokes with gold ribbons circling the base of the filters. He removed one, placed it in his mouth, and paused, letting it dangle between his lips. Harry lit the end with his lighter as Dad inhaled deeply. The red tip rose up and glowed. The men were captivated, and Dad held them in rapture. He exhaled, allowing the smoke to dissipate in front of him. Then he handed the cigarette to the man who had so violently pounded the hood of our car. Dad lit another, and another, and another. By the time the last Dunhill was distributed, it was as if a magic spell had been cast. And an even vaster silence descended.

I must have entered a trance myself, because when Mom tapped my knee, a tall imposing Sikh stood next to Dad, addressing the crowd on the side of the road. His white turban was knotted tightly and his dark suit was immaculately pressed. He pulled his arms through the air in front of him as if he was smoothing a cover over a bed, and he closed and reopened his eyes very slowly. The men stepped away from him as he spoke. Some turned and returned to the field, dragging their sickles in the dirt. Others stayed and talked with the Sikh, pointing with their sharp tools to a place on the side of the road behind our car where a child was hit. One man gestured ahead, far into the distance.

Dad rounded the car as the Sikh continued in conversation, and Mom rolled down her window. "This man speaks perfect English. He will take you and Jane to Agra," Dad said in a husky whisper. His breath smelled vile. Dad reached deep into the pocket of his pants for his wallet and shoved it into Mom's hand. When he kissed her forehead, he strained a smile and said, "You'll be alright, baby. I love you. Chin up."

Harry had already lifted the wheelchair from the trunk. Once Mom transferred into it, the four of us crossed over the road to where the Sikh had parked his car. It was identical to ours: a cream-colored exterior and light-beige tufted interior, an elongated hood and a high step up to enter. An elderly woman sat in the back seat and when we opened the door, she didn't smile and barely glanced our way. She wore a navy blue knit suit and her gray hair was twisted into a bun at the nape of her neck, her hands folded in her lap. She stared into the leather on the back of the driver's seat as I helped Mom shift into the touring car. I fumbled over Mom's leg brace and took my place between the two of them.

The old woman lifted her chin as Dad kissed Mom. I couldn't look him in the eye. Would I ever see Dad again?

"Be strong," Mom said, as our new driver scrambled into his seat and accelerated toward Agra. I reached for her hand, and she grabbed mine at the same time. It was hard to tell who was lending strength to whom until we wove our fingers together in a mutual grasp.

"We will make a stop up this way," the new driver said as we set off down the road. He pointed straight ahead and then curved his hand hesitantly to the left as if he were trying to envision a turnoff he'd never noticed before. He spoke with a precise British accent that brought a sense of order along with it. "In this next village," he said, "we shall pick up the injured child and get her proper medical attention." His words prickled in my ear, against my face. So we did hit a child. How did it get to the village ahead of us? We hadn't seen anything. "It's a young girl," he said. "You are lucky. Quite lucky, in fact. Girls don't matter much in these rural communities. It is only the boys that really count."

He leaned into the steering wheel and told us that our first driver had also been removed to this village where we were headed. "He's a brother Muslim," our driver said. "Don't worry. He will endure." But had it been a boy that we injured, our driver shook his head, the story would be quite different. "It's the Indian countryside," he said. "This is nowhere for you to be."

Nowhere to be. Where should we be? And where were we

going now with this all-knowing Sikh and his prim elderly passenger? And how could we have left Dad and Harry alone on the side of the road with all those men with their sharp instruments? Why didn't we insist that they come with us? Had we abandoned them the way our driver had abandoned us? We were little specks in the universe. We were tiny particles, dust on the horizon of a giant world, insignificant passengers on a smoky road in the middle of nowhere. Nowhere we should be. Nobody knew where we were. I'd never felt so small and insignificant. It was becoming a struggle to fill my miniature lungs. Until that moment, I had never really thought about death.

The father was crouched outside of a lean-to, waiting for us, cradling his injured daughter in his arms. The girl was thin and gangly, maybe five years old, in a faded floral-print dress. Her arms were crossed over her chest and her legs fell limp from her father's embrace, dangling toward the earth. I saw her blink. She was alive. Her chest raised and lowered. She was *alive!* But how alive?

Father and daughter settled into the front seat beside our driver, and we backed down the dirt path until we reached the main road to Agra. A grimy smell of smoke and sweat filled the interior. I could hear the father's wheezing, but I couldn't see his face. Then, unexpectedly, he twisted one of his shoulders, and looked directly at me. His eyes were sunken deep beneath his brow and his chest heaved when he clenched his jaw and exhaled, pushing out deep-sounding vibrations that began low in his throat. I returned his gaze. He was a young man, probably Harry's age, and his beard was thick and dark, like Harry's. His hair fell onto his forehead and into his eyes like a boy's. I tried to empty myself of all thought and soften my eyes to express compassion.

But the man hardened his with steely determination. He seethed and peered. I thought of his wounded spirit. I thought, again, of those dancing bears— trapped with chained legs, removed from their homes and separated from everything that was familiar to them. I wondered if this father had ever ridden in a luxury car like this or seen American women so close up. He was ensnared in our world now.

Or were we the trapped ones? We were the intruders; our car was the culprit, after all. Now I felt certain that I could die here at the hands of this inconsolable father. He fixated his attention on me and wouldn't look away. Clearly, he wanted to take my life as an act of revenge: one young girl in exchange for another. I stared into my lap, powerless, until my fear dissolved into curiosity. What if it were so? What if this really was the end? Only one thought came clearly to mind: I would never fall in love or know craving desire. I was fifteen and all I yearned for was physical love. This seemed absurd. Shouldn't I be afraid of loss or of the painful separation from my family? My friends? But I was not afraid of death. I was distraught that I might die before I ever loved.

The Red Cross sign tacked to the side of a building forced my mind back into focus. That international symbol of disaster relief shone vibrant and welcoming in this remote and dusty setting. We had veered yet again into a village off the road. This community had a central paved road and a small hospital built from cinder blocks. But there were no people on the street this late afternoon. Why? Our driver parked the car under the Red Cross sign, left its motor running, and darted from his seat to escort the father and daughter into the brick building. Did he rush because he was worried about the survival of the girl? If so, which girl?

Not even a minute had passed when he rushed back out from the building, jumped into the car, and threw the vehicle into reverse, dirt flying in all directions. But this time the sound of tire rubber burning against the pavement signaled the terrifying level of danger we were escaping from. It was turning dark outside. A hush filled the car, thick and uniform like Jell-O. Nobody spoke for a long while. Everything that was important was unknown. Would the girl survive? Would she be crippled for life? Where were Dad and Harry? What would Mom and I do once we made it to Agra? And who was this woman beside us?

"Sometimes we are not in control," the woman in the knit suit said, breaking the silence and speaking for the first time. "Sometimes we must surrender to circumstance." She was a widow, she told us. And she had a son who had disappeared on this road in India four years earlier. She was retracing her child's route, not because she believed she would miraculously find him, but because she hoped she might come to understand him better. "The loss is devastating," she said. "It can be hard to take the next step."

I scooted closer to Mom and lined my hip up next to hers, pushed my leg into the metal of her brace. And what if we didn't die on this road? Then what? How would we carry on together?

We arrived at our hotel as night was falling and found a steep flight of stairs leading up to its entrance. Mom bit her lower lip, then reached into her purse for a lipstick. I squinted to count the stairs as our driver ascended to the lobby to check on our reservations.

"We can do this, Mom," I said.

"I'm not good at surrendering," she said and snapped her purse closed.

We waited silently.

"Do you see what I see?" I asked Mom, who was filing papers into the zipper pocket of her purse, searching for Ellen Roy's telephone number in New Delhi. She looked up as Dad and Harry skipped down the steps two at a time, bounding toward us.

"Baby!" Dad shouted and his smile was wider than I had ever seen it. He flung open the car's door. "We all made it!" Mom reached up toward him and Dad dropped to his knees and pressed his face into her chest.

Agra, India
February 9, 1970

"The Taj Mahal is the world's most famous monument to love," declared our guide. Shah Jahan, the seventeenth-century Mogul emperor, commissioned the mausoleum in memory of his favorite of three wives, who died in childbirth. He began a detailed explanation of the inlay techniques perfected by the shah's artisans when Mom politely interrupted him. "We are exhausted from traveling," she said. "My family would like to rest in the gardens for a while."

I hadn't slept the night before. Once we had settled into our hotel, Dad and Harry told Mom and me the story of how they escaped from the men on the roadside. The crowd dissipated, they said, once Mom and I left the scene. The Sikh had shamed the men into releasing Mom and me into his custody: "What kind of village is this that holds women and children hostage? Where is your honor? Your decency as men?" he had asked. He promised the village leader that he would deliver the injured girl to a hospital for care. Harry and Dad shared a second pack of cigarettes with the men who lingered after we left, and when Dad noticed a car traveling in the direction of Agra, he and Harry darted toward it and hitched a ride to the city. They were never informed about what happened to our first driver, and they never learned about the injuries to the child.

Mom gave me a sleeping pill, but it didn't keep me from kicking the sheets on my bed all night. I was afraid that the men Dad and Harry left behind would track us down and break into our hotel and take revenge, kidnap us, kill us. I was afraid our first driver had been murdered on the spot and that it was our fault entirely. I didn't think about the fate of the little girl. I couldn't allow myself to think about that. But I thought about her father and his haunting glare, an image I couldn't shake. We were innocent, I reminded myself. It wasn't our fault! We weren't driving the car! We were just sightseers! Tourists!

Unless we *were* responsible. If not for us, that fancy rambling car would never have been traveling down that dusty road to Agra. I wondered if our very presence was a disturbance. Were we invaders carrying a curse of modernization like the new sanitary systems that caused polio?

A rectangular reflecting pool stretched through the gardens in front of the Taj Mahal, and tourists had gathered at the top end of it for photographs. The setting was a perfect backdrop for a magazine-like image. We waited with other families, and when it was our turn, Dad posed Mom and me in front of the water. Mom sat erect in her chair and I stood to her side, resting my hand on her handlebars. But I didn't really feel like being a tourist and didn't want to pretend to be amused at the marvelous sight. The morning sun glared into my face, and I squinted, reliving the experience of our accident.

"Smile," Dad instructed me. "This is one of the world's greatest shots!" He took a few steps backward to get a grander view. "You know," he shook his head. "I can't really capture it."

We passed a boy at the main gate as we left the grounds of the Taj Mahal. He was a teenager, about my age, wrapped in a loose white cloth. He was propped up on a pile of tattered pillows and his exposed bony legs were folded in front of him on a mat as if set out as an offering. One of his hands was extended, begging. One of his legs hung limp and atrophied. Just like the boy's in the park in New Delhi. And like the young girl's. And like Mom's.

I let go of the side rail on Mom's wheelchair, and she continued with Dad and Harry down the sidewalk toward the exit gate. I reached into my shoulder bag for some rupees. The boy didn't look at me when I kneeled to place the coins in his hand, and I knew that I was just another tourist to him, a passing speck of dust. But I paused there for a moment, anyway, and shared his silence. And as I headed for the gate to catch up with my family, from behind me, I heard a moan.

SEVEN

Kabul, Afghanistan
February 15, 1970

THE TAXI DRIVER AT THE Kabul International Airport leaned his backside against the passenger door of his putty-colored Moskvitch and picked at his cuticles, avoiding eye contact with Mom and me on the curb in front of him. A bus lumbered up behind him and screeched to a halt, and Mom and I watched the other passengers who'd gotten off our Air India flight drag their suitcases up the stairs into its cabin. All the passengers boarded and the bus rambled off, leaving a cloud of thick exhaust hanging in the air.

Mom coughed into the back of her hand. "I'm not sure I'd want to take that bus even if I could," she said. "You can suffocate from that kind of soot."

Dad was inside the terminal exchanging Indian rupees for local Afghan currency and Harry had wheeled the dolly with our luggage over to the end of the sidewalk where he stood gazing up into the mountains at a distance. I looked over at the taxi driver, who was wearing a gray lambskin hat—pointy, like the paper boats I folded with the pages from my notebook during study hall, only upside down. He glanced at Mom's chair, circled his eyes suspiciously around the rim of her wheel, and then returned to the job of grooming his fingers.

Dad swung open the terminal doors and walked toward the driver. "Good afternoon," he smiled. "We're going to the Hotel Intercontinental, please. Can you give us a ride?"

The driver lifted his hat from the back of his head and shoved it low on his brow but didn't respond verbally.

"Inter. Continental," Dad said slowly.

"Da. Da," the man responded and shook his head "No" as he looked down at his shoes.

"Show him this, Sol." Mom snapped open her purse and located our hotel reservations typed out on the Kabul Intercontinental letterhead. "The hotel is brand-new. It just opened. He might not know the address."

But the driver didn't budge after he scanned the paper, and Dad folded the reservation back up and returned inside the air terminal.

"Oh well." I shrugged as if there were nothing disturbing about the fact that we might be stranded at this airport. We were used to logistical problems, weren't we? "At least we aren't in India anymore!" I cheered.

Not physically, anyway. But mentally, I surely had not moved on. I was still scared that those men from the village on the road to Agra would mysteriously track our family down and seek revenge. We had left India in a hurry, several days earlier than we had planned, and we hadn't learned the prognosis of the injured girl. I couldn't let go of all the what-ifs that replayed in my mind like a scratched vinyl record. What if Dad and Harry had never escaped from the side of the road on the way to Agra? What if Mom and I were left there on our own, suddenly a family of two? What if we had hit a boy and not a girl with our car? What if Mom and I had been taken hostage with the Sikh and the lady in the navy knit suit? What if the little girl had died? I dropped my grip on Mom's handlebars and wrapped my arms around my waist. I had suffered with a stomachache for days.

Dad returned from the terminal again, this time with an employee from Air India by his side. The man wore the same uniform that our attendant in Rome had, and he held himself in the same officious manner—head lifted, shoulders squared, sniffy. But this time I found reassurance in those shiny brass buttons and the waxed mustache that covered his mouth. There was authority in his footsteps' clipped tempo, and I felt encouraged when I recognized that he was our ally. I smiled at him and rearranged my hair: I'd never found a uniform comforting before. It's funny how quickly impressions can change.

The man from Air India approached the taxi driver. He had stepped away from his car and now he lowered his hands to his side like a soldier at attention. The two men were about the same height, and they stood close together, leaning into one another, speaking quietly at first. But soon they became agitated, tapping their chests and raising their hands, palms up, toward the sky. Dad, who had been standing beside them, stepped backward onto the curb and shoved his fists into his pants pockets until the yelling stopped. The man from Air India approached Dad. He held his head low, and Dad closed his eyes and rubbed his temples as they talked. Dad came over to Mom and leaned over the rails of her wheelchair to explain the situation: Disease is considered bad luck, a curse in this part of the world. The driver doesn't want a wheelchair in his car because he thinks the bad luck of illness will spread from his taxi to his family. These kinds of superstitions are widespread here, and we are going to have trouble finding any transportation—

But before Dad could finish his explanation, the uniformed man returned to his side and placed a hand on his shoulder. "We have reached an agreement and the driver will take you to the hotel now," he said. "He will not have it be said that he showed disrespect for visitors. For women and for children." He yanked at his starched shirt cuff and asked Dad: "Can your wife walk?"

"Let's go on with this while there's an opening," Mom said, handing me her purse before she unlocked the brakes on her chair.

Mom settled into the front seat of the Moskvitch and Dad collapsed the wheelchair and maneuvered it into the car's trunk, where it took up the entire space.

"For God's sake," Dad said. "What the hell do we do with the luggage?"

"Let me get Harry," I said.

Harry was finishing a smoke, facing the mountains with his back toward us, and seemed oblivious to the tense situation.

"We need you," I said.

The two of us started down the sidewalk, Harry rolling the luggage cart, but I didn't get the chance to tell him about the problem with the taxi driver because Dad started shouting at us from down the curb: "For crying out loud, Harry. Pick it up, will you? Get your ass in gear!"

Harry dropped his cigarette to the ground but didn't pick up his pace. Why was Dad so uptight? What's the big hurry about, man? But the driver had already started the engine of his car and was gunning the accelerator when we arrived with the luggage and Dad was wiping sweat from his forehead.

"We've got to split up," Dad said and handed Harry some money. "Find a second cab and follow us to the Intercontinental. Take the bags."

"Cool," Harry said. "We'll caravan. That's what they do in the Hindu Kush."

"Oh so clever," Dad replied. "Just watch your wallet while you ride your camel."

Our taxi sputtered away from the airport in fits and starts. The Soviet-made Moskvitch was noticeably insubstantial and tinny, nothing like the posh British tourist cars in India. This one was rusty on the outside and dented in around the headlights; the interior seats were hard like a school bus's and the brown covers were cracked and crusted with dirt. "Proletariat," Dad said as he brushed off his trousers. He pushed his hands up against the cab's ceiling to stabilize himself against the bumps as the car jerked along the highway. Mom gripped the dashboard to keep her balance. I didn't know what *proletariat* meant but I got the idea that the Soviets didn't design for comfort. Dad rolled down his window and the thin mountain air was dry against my face.

The panorama out the window was rough and monochromatic, subtle variations of brown and beige for as far as I could see, with jagged mountains way off on the horizon. There were no people I could spot, no life at all really—except for some goats randomly clustered in the dust. But the sky! The cloudless sky was the color of polished lapis lazuli, so intense that it made my eyes water. I squinted to focus on the treeless mountains, far away. Absence. There was nothing here. It was a landscape defined by what was missing from it. Was there even wind in this stripped-away place?

We passed through the still and soundless countryside for what seemed like half an hour until some mud buildings began to crop up near the side of the road and we entered the outskirts of Kabul. People began to appear. A group of men huddled together on stools at the doorway of a teahouse, hunched over in a circle and talking with their hands. They were dressed in loose kaftans and wool vests and their heads were wrapped in circles of off-white cloth. They looked up as our car sputtered by. Their faces were deep-creased and wind-worn. They had character, I thought; the kind of faces that made me think of biblical patriarchs—wise and wizened and humorless. Where were the women? I searched around, but the faces of women were missing.

Bright-colored forms sprang up on the streets when we reached the center of the city. The first one I noticed was canary yellow, and it scurried out through the glass door of a two-story office build-ing and rushed down the sidewalk. The lively yellow was a happy surprise in this drab environment, but the total concealment was shocking. This was a woman? Why did she cover herself like that? What was she concerned about? "Burkas," Mom said, looking at me from the side of her eyes as if she had a story to tell me. "For modesty." She smirked. I noticed other paint-box-colored burkas on the sidewalk—periwinkle blue, apple green, cherry red like the color of Mom's lipstick. The burkas were tightly pleated and hung over the heads of the anonymous silhouettes. When the thin cloth fell to the ground, it spread like a fan and flapped in the dust on the sidewalks. No arms. No legs. No facial expressions or clues of per-sonality could be discerned. The women were unseeable, hidden under distracting colors that called attention to their invisibility.

"Mom?"

"Imagine—" she said and tsked without turning to see my face.

Dad rolled up the car window as we pulled into an intersection and stopped at a traffic light. "I wonder who's behind the drapes," he chuckled. "How do you suppose you know who you're talking to?"

And who gave these women permission to walk up to our idling taxi and stare at us through the windows? Four or five of them stood inches away from the closed car window, pushing their bodies against each other and rounding their heads in our direction. They peered through the embroidered grillwork that shielded their faces, and I could feel the penetrating gazes, even though I couldn't see their eyes. The women huddled and lingered, and I felt disapproval in their fixed attention, but I didn't know why. Was it their silent proximity that made me so uneasy? Was it their anonymity that granted them the license to so boldly encroach? Maybe they were just curious about our Western appearance, and they intended no harm in their breach of our privacy. I covered the back of my neck with my hand. In the presence of these concealed women, I felt exposed and self-conscious, and yet something about them reminded me of myself.

I remembered the sense of power that I felt as a two-year-old, when I hid under the bed sheets at the Lido Motel and stared into the hub of Mom's wheel. I peered out into our room, but no one could see me. Hidden like that, I had captured my parents' undivided attention. It was an act of rebellion to hide myself away, and I wielded important influence by refusing to reveal myself. Did these women feel the same way? Were they strengthened by their cover-ups? By the ability that they possessed to stalk and haunt?

I peered back at the array of colorful silhouettes crouching beside our door and focused my attention on the bright blue burka that was closest to the window. What did she look like? Could she possibly be my age? Would she shy away from staring so intently if

I could see her eyes? I couldn't penetrate her stonelike stance. I narrowed my eyes, annoyed by her presence: Go away! This is unfair! Leave me alone! But she didn't budge. She was shielded from my rebuke and stood planted in place, resolute, like the distant mountain peak beyond her on the horizon.

"Today is a holiday," the desk clerk informed us when we checked into our hotel. Most of the city was closed in observance, he told us, but everything in the hotel was open for our enjoyment. Harry set out on foot to explore the neighborhood around the hotel and Dad headed immediately to the gym in the basement to unwind in the steam bath. Mom and I relaxed beside the giant picture window that dominated the hotel lobby. The hotel was perched on a hilltop overlooking the city and the view was undisturbed. The oversized lobby was as empty as the landscape. We ordered drinks from the bar.

I took a seat beside Mom and stuffed a pillow behind the small of my back. The cushion was oversized like everything else. It was stitched together patchwork from pieces of old woven carpets. I felt at ease for the first time in days when I leaned into its firm and luxurious support. Thick-looped tassels hung from its side and I folded my legs up into a lotus position. "Kabul's pretty from here, isn't it, Mom?" I asked. "There's something so calm about these neutral colors."

"Desolate," Mom said, and she reached for her scotch and soda. "This isn't a part of the world that too many people ever see."

"And you don't even see the women at all," I said. I was thinking about the one we left behind, standing in the street in her bright blue burka. She and I had communicated for sure, but the exchange was unsettling—it felt more like a standoff than an understanding. It bothered me that I couldn't read her face. There might have been nothing more than curiosity in that woman's presence, but I had no way of telling. I took a sip of Coke and the carbonation fizzed into my eyes.

"Are you all right?" Mom asked.

"I just wonder what it's like to be one of those covered-up women. They walk around like they're invisible. It's kind of scary. Like they really don't exist. But they do. And they sort of don't. I mean, in India you could see the women's faces even though they were wrapped in scarves. I thought they looked beautiful."

I watched the bubbles escape from my Coke and pop into the air. I was interested in what Mom thought about these women, because so often people treated her as if she was invisible. But Mom was unusually quiet and seemed distracted by other thoughts. She unzipped her purse and reached for her green leather travel journal, staring into middle space as she ran her finger along the book's curved corner. I imagined she was considering which of our recent travel episodes she wanted to record. Maybe it was the problem with the superstitious taxi driver that had left her troubled.

"Sweetheart," she said after a long pause. "There's something I'd like to share with you." Mom thumbed through the gold-rimmed pages of her little book and twisted her mouth to one side as if she were contemplating the wisdom of continuing with her revelation.

I flinched when I heard the word share. When Mom said share, I heard pry. I could tell by the thoughtful way she was handling her journal that she was about to broach a sensitive subject. What could it be? Was she still mulling over the incident with the child on the road to Agra? Did she want to talk about what we might do if we were ever separated from Dad and Harry again? Separation, always, was her greatest worry. Abandonment. Helplessness. But I didn't want to discuss her anxieties right now. I grabbed my glass and rattled the ice cubes around. I just wanted to space out and absorb the unobstructed view of Kabul.

"Remember that palm reader in New Delhi?" Mom asked, still flipping through the pages of her journal. "He was a very interesting man."

I forced out an exaggerated sigh that started deep in my belly. That little man in a dark shiny suit with bulging unfocused eyes had come to our suite at the Oberoi. The Guptas, business contacts of Mom and Dad's who owned a company that distributed car tires, had arranged the meeting. "He's very good," Mrs. Gupta had promised, her gold bangles jangling as she fiddled with the folds of her sari. "We consult him very often." He was their banker, she explained, who advised on business concerns during the day and on personal matters after hours.

Mom had been instantly intrigued. "It is an age-old tradition here," she said to Dad and flashed him a playful smile. "Soothsayers."

When he arrived at our room, disheveled and with a portfolio shoved under his arm, Harry and I rolled our eyes. How could anyone take this funny-looking man seriously? He reminded me of Mr. Magoo, the nearsighted goofball cartoon character. Perfect, I thought, a seer with bad vision!

"I found that that banker was very insightful," Mom continued, sitting in the lobby of the Intercontinental.

I pulled the pillow from behind my back and plopped it into my lap, where its heavy weight felt good against my stomach. When that man placed my hands faceup in his and ran his index finger down the center of my palm, I had to suppress a giggle. His light touch tickled, but more than that, I felt awkward with him, behind a closed door. Mom and Dad and Harry were waiting together on the door's other side, but the fact remained that this odd fellow was fondling my hands, and nobody could see us. When he told me that I would face "some difficult choices" as I grew up, I pulled my palms back and slapped them down on the table between us: And who doesn't have tough choices to make? He smiled. "Ah," he said. "I see that you are a skeptic. This is very, very good. You could have a very good life in front of you." I left the room, perplexed as to how anyone could fall for his nonsense.

But Mom did. She spent longer than expected behind that closed door as Dad and Harry and I waited for her to finish. We cracked jokes about the man's craftiness. Harry thought the man was a complete fraud. Dad scoffed: "It's a great business he has going there," he said. "Really. No inventory to worry about. All he needs to do is find a sucker and show up and start talking." I wondered how Mom could stand it, and yet, I had to admit, I was slightly curious as to what he might be telling her.

"I thought he was creepy," I said to Mom as I looked out the window over Kabul. "His comments were so general. They could apply to anyone. He told me that I would have choices to make."

"Well, he was very specific with me," Mom said. By now she had folded back the binding of her journal and was tapping her finger at a specific passage.

"Like what?" I asked with half-feigned interest.

"He thought Harry was too cynical, that's one thing," Mom said. "He said Harry would have to overcome his deep negative way of thinking in order to be successful." She read from her journal pages: Harry will be more famous than wealthy. At age thirty he will work as an adviser to a large company.

"So stupid," I said. "Mom, the man was ridiculous. Anyone can look at Harry and tell that he's a rebel."

"He thought I stayed too much in my head," Mom said, turning over a page. "He told me I think too much about the future and need to stay in the now. In the present. But he thinks I'm very lucky."

"Sounds like good advice. The part about not thinking too much," I said. "But did you tell him that you liked to worry?" I smiled.

Mom stuck a finger in her journal and closed its cover. "To be a mother is to worry," she said, looking deeply into my eyes. "My mother taught me that."

It was true that Mom and Grandma were both chronic worriers, but I never understood that it had much to do with having children. They had each suffered serious trauma that left them unsure of themselves. I always thought Grandma's nervous personality was a result of being orphaned as a young girl in Russia. And Mom constantly worried about her physical safety and her limited ability to function independently. Both of them worried about themselves. None of that had anything to do with being a mother.

"Well, you are lucky," I said. "Look where you are right now! On top of the world!" I gestured out the window at the vast openness in front of us, hoping to change the subject. The blue tint of the sky had muted, and striations of gentle tints were beginning to intensify. It was hard to imagine a more inspirational setting—this uninterrupted view into what looked like eternity. "I don't think it looks like a moonscape anymore," I said. "It's more like a painter's palette. Look how the colors are mixing together. They change so fast. I think we're in for a show."

"One day you'll understand," Mom said, without glancing out the window at the view. She sucked in her red lower lip. "He spent most of his time talking about you, Jane."

I covered the side of my neck with my hand, just like I did in the car when I felt the forceful gaze of the burka-covered women. "I'm not sure I want to hear any more, Mom. You're taking this stuff too seriously for me," I said. The pillow tassels had gotten tangled up in my lap and I started separating out the strands.

"Maybe so," she said. "But he said he thought you were at peace with yourself. You have a good sense of who you are." Mom read from her journal: Jane recently experienced a tragedy in travel, and it has deeply affected the way she thinks.

Why did that man choose me to pay attention to? Wasn't the rest of the family more interesting? Couldn't he have pondered Mom's layers of emotional complexity or Dad's stubborn good-naturedness? And Harry! There was a character whose contrarian attitude was worthy of his examination! But me? What was there to say about a dutiful daughter who liked to be left to her own devices?

"He said you don't recognize how smart you are."

"Oh great," I said and tugged at one of the tassels until I tore the stitching, and it came loose in my hand.

Mom read again from her leather book: Jane's strong family ties will hold her back. But now she avoided my eyes and finally looked out the window into the nascent sunset. She rubbed the tip of her nose and began to blink rapidly. Oh, Mom. Please don't start to cry. She looked stiff and thin-armed, as if she were trapped in her wheelchair and was too frail to move away. Come on, Mom, please. But I didn't reach over and place my hand on her knee to reassure her of my support. I kept myself at a distance and adjusted the pillow in my lap.

"You're worried about me?" I finally asked.

I wondered what deep chord that soothsaying banker had touched in her. Had he said more than what Mom was divulging?

My chest tightened. I couldn't begin to unravel the layers of Mom's anxiety. But more than that, I realized that I didn't really want to.

The colors of the sunset intensified. The soft striations that were heliotrope and gray just moments ago had merged and transformed into a gust of burning orange, filling the whole sky as if the world had been set on fire. "Wow, Mom," was all I thought to say. "Wow."

I knew she worried about me. She made that perfectly clear. She thought I was distant, too detached, unreachable, too private. "Talk to me," she would plead back in Dallas. "Turn off those Beatle records and talk to me! I'm your mother!" But most of the time I had nothing I wanted to say. I found equilibrium in my silence, and I lost myself in music. If she would just leave me alone. Couldn't she understand that I wanted to be helpful, tending to her physical needs—but at the same time I needed room for myself. Couldn't she see that my time alone was important? I needed latitude to gain independence.

I watched Mom's face tighten as she sipped her scotch and soda. We were so closely entwined that I couldn't figure out where her needs ended and where mine began. But as deeply as we resonated together, there was also a serious disconnect. I didn't think Mom understood the impact that her physical needs had on me. If she did, she never acknowledged it. The topic was too big, I supposed, so it was set aside. Just like I never explained how I pulled away from her in order to preserve myself. I never occurred to me that I could refuse to help her. "Mom, I'm busy right now," was not an attitude I was able to embrace. She was my mother! How could I leave her helpless? That goofy little man in India had touched on a dissonance that neither of us wanted uncovered: *Jane's strong family ties will hold her back.*

Mom and I placed our empty glasses on the table in front of us and they remained there, like a still life, until a waiter leaned over and removed them on a tray. We stayed still ourselves, having retreated into our separate worlds, each of us staring into vacant space. For a long moment, I thought about that woman in her bright blue burka and I envied her—shielded from view, protected from inspection, her identity preserved, and her privacy intact. I hesitated before I reached for Mom's hand and squeezed it. I motioned with my chin to the breathtaking beauty of the sky out our window, ablaze.

I was up all night, heaving into the toilet of the marble-floored bathroom that Harry and I shared. I became lightheaded as I emptied my stomach. Mucus dripped from my nose and tears seeped from the corners of my eyes. I stripped off my clothes and beads of sweat dripped from my armpits and dropped from my hairline to the tip of my chin. The wretched smell triggered a cycle of responses as I vomited and vomited and vomited.

Harry was convinced I got food poisoning from the dinner we ate in the hotel's coffee shop.

"That wonderful hamburger you had was probably horse meat," he called out to me from the bedroom.

Or maybe it was the hashish we smoked before we went down for that meal. Earlier that evening, after the sun had set, Dad joined Mom in the hotel lobby all pink-cheeked and chipper from his steam bath. "Tired, baby?" he asked as he squeezed Mom's shoulder. I left them alone and retreated to my room, where Harry was resting on his bed, ankles crossed, reading a *Cambridge History of the Ancient World*.

"I've got something to show you," he said when I plopped onto my bed. He pulled a wad of tin foil the diameter of a silver dollar from the front pocket of his Levi's and held it out in front of him between his thumb and index finger. Harry grinned.

"I met some Peace Corps volunteers at a teahouse down the road here. We hung out and watched the sunset. Unbelievable sunset. And look what I scored from them." He waved the wad of tin foil in front of his face. "Afghani hash. The purest stuff in the world."

In India, Harry and I had smoked hashish that he bought from some students he met at the hotel disco. He and I sat on the floor of our hotel room in New Delhi and smoked it as we listened to sitar music from the radio console between our beds. It was powerful; so strong that I couldn't lift my legs from the floor after a few inhalations. I stared at my feet and tried to wiggle my toes until I finally fell asleep on the carpet. I was used to lightweight weed that I rolled into joints and smoked with my friends in Dallas—weed that gave me a slight buzz but was more likely a mixture of basil and oregano from the grocery than marijuana from Mexico. I wasn't used to real drugs, or to getting high with Harry.

"I don't know if I really want to smoke that stuff tonight," I said to Harry when he suggested we try his hashish before going down to the lobby for dinner. "I'm pretty tired." I didn't want to share with Harry the conversation I'd just finished with Mom about the palm reader in India. I was still churning through my mind just what Mom was trying to communicate. *Jane's family ties will hold her back.* Is that what she wanted for me? Is that what she feared? Worried about? I knew that if I tried to talk to Harry about what Mom had said he would dismiss the whole thing: "Screw her," I imagined he'd say. "She's just trying to put a guilt trip over on you."

"Harry?" I asked instead. "Do you think I'm always going to be a mommy's girl?"

Harry lit up a pipe of hashish, inhaled, and handed me the bowl without answering. I took in a long drag and held the smoke in my lungs until I burst out in laughter.

AMERICAN HAMBURGER was printed in bold Times New Roman on the laminated menu of the hotel's coffee shop. "Yummy!" I said to Harry as my mind pulled me back to Big Boy's in Dallas— double patties with mustard and pickles on a Wonder Bread bun and the salty taste of greasy French fries. "Let's get cheeseburgers," I said.

"I'm not sure," Harry said. "We are in Afghanistan, remember."

"Exactly," I smiled, my eyelids drooping over my dilated eyes. "It's not India. We can eat meat!"

A serving of ground meat the shape of a tennis ball appeared before me. It was garnished with chopped herbs and centered on top of a piece of buttered flatbread. Thick triangular wedges that looked something like potatoes were arranged in a careful circle at the rim of the plate and little glass cups filled with mustard and ketchup were set off to the side of the plate. Not quite the Big Boy I had envisioned, but the meatball had the aroma of a Texas T-bone. I carved into it enthusiastically with a fork and serrated knife.

"I swear, Harry, and it's not because I'm high. This is the best hamburger I've ever eaten." Harry ate his lamb kebab on rice and didn't ask for a taste of my burger.

One hour later, the vomiting began.

I ordered dry toast the next morning for breakfast. Mom commented that my face looked pale, and I told her that I had been up all night with a violent stomachache.

"You know, it could be the altitude," she said. "It's very high here."

"Yeah," Harry laughed as he dribbled syrup over his short stack. "It's really high here, Jane."

"Ha, ha," I said sarcastically. If Mom and Dad had any inkling that Harry and I had smoked hashish in our room, they never gave us a hint of their knowledge.

I nibbled at my toast, but even that had no appeal. I wondered if food would ever taste good again. The waiter brought me a cup of hot tea and I just stared into the clear amber.

"Everyone," I said after a minute of gathering my thoughts. "I have an announcement."

Mom lifted her coffee cup and eyebrows as Dad leaned back in his chair, smiling his amusement at my show of assuredness.

"Now what?" Harry asked.

"I am becoming a vegetarian," I said, wiggling to the front of my seat. "I'm never eating meat again. Ever."

"You know," Dad said. "That's probably a pretty healthy lifestyle. I might join you."

Harry stayed silent and Mom clinked her coffee cup into its saucer.

"Well," she said. "It will be interesting to see where that leads."

EIGHT

Tehran, Iran
February 19–24, 1970

THE EMERALDS ON THE TOP ROW of the tiara were the size of quarters and the shocking green of Astroturf. Just below them, their size lessened to that of dimes. Across the room there was a brooch encrusted with miniature seed pearls that had been woven into the shape of a plum and embedded with rubies. Then there was a red velvet crown with a starburst of diamonds and sapphires next to a jewel-studded sword and shield. A globe twirled on a stand, its seas crafted from emeralds and the landmasses from red rubies. In the back corner a golden throne glowed. These were the crown jewels of Persia, priceless and crammed into glass display cases in the dimly lit basement of the Central Bank of Iran.

"I'm just speechless," Mom said as Dad guided her down a narrow aisle. They stopped in front of a royal shield, and I wandered away, over to the golden throne. It was smaller than I ever imagined a throne would be—the seat not much bigger than that of Mom's wheelchair. The backrest was carved into peacock feathers and the entire chair was covered in gold and inlaid with colorful jewels. A pair of ducks decorated the backrest; a lion with a loopy tail animated the footstool.

Behind the throne's display hung an oversized photograph of Mohammad Reza Pahlavi on the day of his coronation as Shah of Iran, October 26, 1967. He stared into the camera, square-jawed and handsome in a black suit, with a firm and impervious gaze. A turquoise sash draped from his shoulder and his chest was covered with ribbons and amulets. A gold belt held a giant emerald centered at his middle where his navel would be. The shah sat on that very chair before me, holding a golden staff, his crown bursting with diamonds, the throne shimmering behind him.

I was lost in thought about the power of this modern-day shah and didn't notice Harry when he came up beside me near the photograph. When Harry began speaking, it sounded as if he was in the middle of a conversation with somebody else. "So they've been hoarding all of this stuff for centuries," he said. "Remember the Taj Mahal? Well, this is what the inside was filled with. Mogul."

I shook my head ambiguously. I didn't know what Harry was talking about and I didn't want to be distracted by trying to figure out what he meant. "Harry," I said. "Look here. It's incredible. This coronation was only two years ago." I pointed to the picture of the shah.

"It's all currency, Jane. Trade. And it all goes back to the ancient Persian Empire. Cyrus the Great."

"It says here that there are 26,733 jewels in this one throne." I looked back to the chair behind the display glass. Each stone by itself was bedazzling. And the throne looked different to me now that I had seen it occupied—it seemed more alive.

Harry stepped closer to the case and bent in toward the glass. He was quiet and narrowed his eyes. I thought for a moment that he might appreciate the beauty of the chair. But I knew that most likely he was collecting his thoughts for another shot at a history lesson.

"This all represents power and control," he said, bobbing his head. "You really have to understand Cyrus the Great to get this. Five hundred B.C."

When I didn't respond, he continued. "You remember the Purim story about Queen Esther, right?"

Of course I remembered the story of Purim. Esther was the great queen of Persia in the Bible who saved the Jewish people from Haman's destruction. I glanced back at the photograph of the shah. Next to him stood his wife, Empress Farah. Her black hair was swept from her shoulders into an elegant French twist and her long neck was exposed like Cleopatra's. Her thick eyeliner extended toward her temples and her eyes shone like the glossy ink. And her jewels! This was the most exquisite-looking woman I could ever imagine! Surely this was the image of Queen Esther. Or, even better, Queen Vashti!

Purim commemorates the story of the Book of Esther. Every year from preschool until fourth grade, I dressed up in petticoats and put on lipstick to celebrate the festival at our synagogue's carnival. The year I remembered best was when I was six years old.

"Why do I have to be Vashti? Why can't I be Queen Esther?" I had asked Mom, pressing my hips into the rim of her wheel and arching my back. "I'm *always* Queen Esther. *Everybody* is always Queen Esther."

Mom was putting on makeup at her dressing table at our house in Fort Worth. She curled a wand of mascara onto her eyelashes and stared into the mirror.

"Queen Vashti was even more beautiful than Esther," Mom said. When she wrapped her arm around my waist, my back released. Mom had shaped her eyebrows with a dark pencil and outlined her lips in red. She smiled at me all-knowingly, like she had a secret but was waiting to reveal it.

She rummaged through her makeup tray with exaggerated playfulness, making clinking sounds, pushing around cases of lipsticks and face powder. "Let me see here," she said. She spoke slowly, drawing out each word the way she did when she read me Babar. Mom knew how to build suspense, tapping her fingernail on the side of her plastic box. I shuffled my bare feet, anticipating what she might discover. "What would look glamorous on you tonight?" she mused. "Befitting of a Persian queen?"

She found a palette of powdered shadows and dusted pearl blue over my eyelids with her fingertip. Then she wet the tip of a dark pencil with her tongue and pulled a dark line over my lashes as I stood perfectly still by her side.

"Queen Vashti was King Ahasuerus's first wife," Mom said and that was when she stretched the corner of my eye out toward my temple and drew an extravagant curl. I pulled my face away to look into the mirror, and I hardly recognized myself. I looked so grown up and exotic! Mom cupped my cheeks into her palms and held me inches from her face before she kissed my forehead.

I had never heard of Queen Vashti. The Purim story that I learned at Sunday school followed a simple fairy-tale plot with four important characters: Queen Esther, King Ahasuerus, Uncle Mordecai, and the wicked Haman. Long ago in the city of Shushan, Ahasuerus was the powerful King of Persia. He married beautiful Esther, a Jewess. When Haman, the king's evil magistrate, plotted to murder all the Jews in the kingdom, Esther and her Uncle Mordecai foiled the wicked plans. Esther was clever. She prepared a banquet for the king, and it was there that she exposed Haman's despicable intentions. Esther prevailed upon her King to save the Jews, and that's how she rescued our people from destruction. We celebrate the victory with a costume party. End of story. No Queen Vashti.

"Queen Vashti was the queen before Queen Esther," Mom said, and she dropped her hands from my face and kept her eyes focused on mine. "You see, there was another aspect to King Ahasuerus," she said. "One evening, he ordered Vashti to entertain him in public and requested that she dance in his court. But he wanted her to dance without clothes on. Completely naked."

I swallowed and looked away from Mom. What? Did the Bible really have a story about naked women? I wasn't interested in the answer and didn't want to hear any more. The story I knew was fine the way I learned it. I just wanted to dress up like Queen Esther and be like everybody else at the Purim carnival. But Mom continued.

"Vashti refused to entertain the king that way," she said. "She was willful. Courageous. She stood up for herself before the king. Vashti dug her knuckles into her waist and raised her chin and looked the King directly in the eye. She said: 'No! I refuse to do that!'"

Why was Mom complicating the story? Why was she so excited about Vashti? What was it about "No!" that was so important to my mother?

"Queen Vashti was the world's first *feminist*," Mom said and the way she pronounced it made it sound like it was in a foreign word—three strong syllables. "King Ahasuerus was furious and banished her from the kingdom because she disobeyed him. It was only after Vashti left that he decided to marry Esther. That's where your Sunday school story begins." Mom brushed my bangs away from my eyes and twisted my hair into a tight bun, securing it to the top of my head with bobby pins. "Ask Rabbi Garsek," she urged as she jabbed extra pins into my scalp. "See what he has to say about Queen Vashti."

But I never asked our rabbi. When we arrived at the synagogue that evening, I met my school friends and we lined up in the front-row pews with our identical pop-bead necklaces and sling-backed plastic high heels. Rabbi Garsek announced the Queen Esther parade and all the other girls pranced before the congregation. I stayed in my seat with the boys—the Hamans and the Mordecais and the King Ahasueruses. I was the only girl that wasn't an Esther.

Mom and Dad sat a few rows behind me. I twisted in my seat to catch a glimpse of them. Mom's wheelchair was parked in the aisle so that she was separated from the other congregants and Dad held her hand from his seat in the pew. They grinned at me, proud-looking and bemused. Mom looked queenlike to me—erect and removed, sturdy in her unique metal chair. She stood out, above the others. And she glowed. An odd sense of confidence overcame me. I felt more special too, distinguished from the other girls—set apart. I liked being the singular Queen Vashti. I couldn't articulate it then, but I learned something that night about the power of defiance, self-assurance. I sat alone and my authority grew.

—

Empress Farah didn't focus into the camera lens like her husband, the shah. She looked slightly off center, at an invisible horizon. There was determination in that askance glance. Was she making her beauty available while guarding her spirit with that distant gaze? Was that aloofness, in fact, her allure? And her emerald crown— was it armor more than adornment? I thought about Queen Vashti and smiled. Maybe she wasn't so wise to stand on principle and lose her authority in the royal court. Would Vashti have done better for herself to look askance like the Empress and try reasoning with the King: *I will dance for you, your Highness, but I will keep by clothes on and remain true to myself.* Isn't that what Esther did? Vashti was defiant and abandoned the palace. Esther was more crafty. She stayed by the king's side and developed her own power. Esther became a triumph. Which response required more strength? I looked closer at Empress Farah's portrait. So often I, too, stared at an undetermined horizon, half engaged and half removed, partly visible and partly disguised. Was the equilibrium I sought a growing source of strength or a symptom of my confusion?

A few days after we visited the crown jewels, Harry and I squeezed our way down a packed sidewalk in the central section of Tehran. We were headed to the station to catch a bus to Isfahan, a two-day overland trip. Mom and Dad would take an airplane and catch up with us there. My overnight clothes were packed into Harry's canvas backpack, and I clung to the straps that hung from it and trailed behind him down the sidewalk. I feared getting lost in that bustle.

Tehran was a hectic, hurried place. Women in miniskirts and heavy makeup clipped down the sidewalk in high heels. The men were clean-shaven and dressed in starched white shirts and dark blazers, swinging briefcases, heading to business meetings. Pop music boomed from stationery shops along the sidewalk. "Yellow Submarine"! There was the smell of fresh bread from food stands and the sound of newspaper hawkers on street corners. I loved the dizzy activity!

Nearer to the bus station, the ambiance slowed, and I let go of the straps on Harry's backpack and walked beside him. We stepped in unison in our blue jeans and Indian sandals, and I knew we stood out as obvious tourists, but I didn't care. I stretched out my stride to keep up with Harry's. I felt safe and protected in my brother's presence, excited to be leaving for an overnight trip.

"Get a load of that!" Harry said and he pointed to a street vendor's stall near the entrance of Tehran's Grand Bazaar. "Looks like halvah to me!"

I looked up at him and licked my lips.

A mound of sandy-colored halvah was stacked in tiers like a wedding cake on a waist-high stand. Our favorite sweet! Sometimes Dad would bring a slice of halvah home from the delicatessen in Fort Worth. He'd buy a chunk of the sesame-seed candy and we'd parcel it out in little squares, nibbling on it for days. It was a special treat, exotic in Texas. Harry and I had never seen such a huge serving of the candy.

The man behind the halvah display chuckled when he noticed the way we were eyeing his tray. "It's very fresh," he called over to us in English. "I can promise you that." He wore a white shirt and pressed black slacks that seemed like a uniform for the men in Tehran. But he had a beard, cropped short like Harry's, and he tugged at the hairs on his chin as he spoke. He and Harry looked very similar. It wasn't only the beard. It was the olive skin and the shadowy deep-set eyes and the relaxed way they held their shoulders. They could be mistaken for cousins, even brothers. "It's delicious," the man said. "Come here, I'll give you a taste." He looked up at Harry and the two of them held each other's gaze longer than most strangers would.

The man used a butcher knife to chip samples off the mound of halvah. He took some pistachios from the top of the heap and sprinkled them over our bites before he handed them to Harry and me on a piece of brown paper. The man's good nature was charming, as soft and gracious as the lilt of his English accent.

The halvah crumbled when I picked it up with my fingers, so I tossed it into my mouth all at once. It stuck to the back of my throat like a wad of peanut butter, and I suctioned it away with my tongue. The salty-sweet confection was oily and gooey but still firm and crunchy. That strange texture was what made it unique, and this halvah seemed tastier than anything we ever got back home. Heavier and stickier, for sure. But was it really? Or was it this atmosphere that made it seem so? The way ice cream is better when you stand in line for it. I shrugged because I knew the answer to my question didn't matter. It was just a lot of fun eating halvah on the street with Harry.

"This is so good," Harry said, picking some crumbs of halvah from his beard. "I really think I could live on this stuff." He poked his hand into the front pocket of his jeans for some coins. "Can you cut us a kilo of that please?"

The salesman smiled. "Are you tourists in Tehran?"

"We're on our way to Isfahan," Harry answered. "This is my little sister."

Our salesman carved a slice from his mound and placed the slab on brown paper wrapping. "Isfahan is my home," he said. "It is very beautiful there. You will like it, I am sure. Are you taking the airplane?"

"We want to see the countryside," Harry said. "We're going by bus."

The man placed our halvah on a plate of his brass scale and rested a one-kilo weight on the countervailing plate. "But the plane is much better for foreigners," he said. He added some pistachios to even out the measurement. "And it is cheap for you." He removed our purchase from his scale and folded creases into the paper, wrapping it carefully. "You need to be very cautious," he said. "The countryside is not like Tehran. You won't find people like me who speak English."

I looked down at my sandals. That was exactly like the warning we received in India. The countryside is no place for tourists. But I didn't say anything. Harry had invited me on this bus trip, and I didn't want him to change his mind about letting me tag along. I stayed quiet and made myself invisible. Something I knew how to do.

"The plane is much better for your sister," the salesman said as he tied twine around our halvah and handed the package to Harry.

"We're all right," Harry said. "Thank you." And he stuffed our candy into the top of his backpack.

The salesman looked over in my direction, but I turned my gaze inward and ignored him.

The bus was first class. The seats were oversized with padded vinyl upholstery and the backs reclined a few inches. But gasoline fumes permeated the cabin, and the air circulation system was weak so that the atmosphere was still and stale. I scooted into a window seat, and Harry took the one next to me on the aisle. As we pulled out of the station, I started to feel closed in.

I was the only female on this bus. The first man who passed down the center aisle stared directly at Harry and nervously averted his eyes from mine when I looked up at him. I recognized the look. There was a childishness about it, like kids at the grocery store who peeped from the side of their eyes at the wheels on Mom's chair, shifting their attention the moment they sensed they were being observed. I realized that I was an oddity—a Western female on an Iranian bus—and it didn't matter to me at first. But by the time the third and fourth man refused to make eye contact with me, I recognized that there was more at stake. I wasn't just strangely out of place; I wasn't welcome among these men. The stares were shunning, and as adept as I was at making myself invisible, I had a hard time disappearing before their harsh glares.

So I looked out the window at the traffic jam on the five-lane highway leading south from Tehran. It was a noisy jumble of cars and buses and trucks, blasting horns and spewing exhaust. Cities everywhere had the same issues, and that notion gave me some inexplicable comfort. The man across the aisle from Harry unwrapped a sandwich and the smell of his seasoned meat overpowered the gas fumes. Behind us someone flipped on a transistor radio. Harry pulled his *Cambridge History* from his backpack and opened it on his lap. I crossed my legs, at ease again.

Traffic gave way to a two-lane highway when we reached the far outskirts of the city and the landscape simplified. Pollution lifted. Mosques and minarets cropped up on the horizon. The men wore loose clothing, no more business blazers and briefcases. They all had short-cropped beards now. Miniskirts and makeup for the women was gone; the few females I saw were wrapped head-to-toe in black.

"This is the *real* Iran," Harry said, gesturing out the window. He closed the book on his lap.

"Yeah?" I said and unfolded my legs. It was beautiful out the window, bright sunshine and open space, clusters of puffy clouds that gathered over scattered groves of palm trees. But Tehran seemed real to me as well. The shah looked real. That halvah salesman, he sure seemed real enough. All those busy people on the downtown streets seemed alive and well as far as I could tell. Why was the countryside suddenly more real than all of that?

"You have to get out with the people. You have to eat where they eat and sleep where they sleep," he said. "Mom just doesn't get it. She loves those giant tourist hotels. But that's not *real*. She doesn't understand travel, Jane."

"Yeah, I know."

I didn't want to contradict Harry, and I understood what he was trying to say. It was wonderful to get out on the road and away from the big city and tourist hotels. But I also felt defensive when Harry was dismissive of Mom. *She doesn't get it.* Harry was too hard on her. As much as I sought independence from Mom, I sympathized with her. Harry didn't know her the same way I did. He didn't fasten her long-line bras or empty her bags of urine. He didn't take her shopping for clothes and protect her from strangers' stares. Harry went to school and studied law; he didn't curl up in bed and listen to Mom's stories about the little redheaded man who lifted her paralyzed legs back onto a gurney in the dark basement of the polio ward in Detroit. *Mom doesn't get it.* Harry didn't appreciate what she had to deal with. *He* didn't get it. Had he forgotten that she couldn't maneuver the narrow hallways and flights of stairs that led to smaller, more "authentic" hotels? How could Harry dismiss the limitations she lived with? And anyway, I think Mom and Dad enjoyed the luxury of fancy hotels.

"Mom and Dad are annoying," I said. "Mom thinks she's so cool. She's always asking me about the lyrics to my Bob Dylan songs. She thinks I don't *share* with her enough."

Harry took the halvah from the top of his backpack and began unwrapping it.

"You ought to share this line with her: *You know something's happening, but you don't know what it is. Do you, Mr. Jones?* That would make her crazy and give her something to think about for a while."

We laughed and Harry handed me a taste of halvah. I filled my mouth with it and didn't say anything. I didn't want to be hard on Mom. I wished she would leave me alone sometimes, but I didn't want to hurt her in the way Harry did. But I definitely didn't want to offend Harry either. He thought Mom was too demanding and self-centered. The two of them were tough on each other and I was trapped in the middle, loyal to both. My hands were oily from the halvah and they reminded me of the pimples that dotted my forehead under my bangs. I pushed down on the bumps trying to flatten them out and make them go away.

"We'll get a good meal tonight," Harry said. "We will be in the ancient city of Qom."

Our bus screeched into the Qom station as the sun was setting. Calls for evening prayer chanted from minarets scattered over the city's landscape. The men around us on the bus grabbed their packages and overnight bags and rushed down the front steps toward the street. Harry and I stayed seated until almost everyone had emptied out and then Harry slung his backpack onto one shoulder, and I followed him down the aisle. The bus driver watched us approach in his rearview mirror and rose as we neared the exit.

"No. No," he said, hanging his head, speaking softly.

"Yes. Yes," Harry retorted, making a move aggressively toward the door.

JANE SAGINAW

"No," the bus driver said, and he stepped directly in front of Harry. "No foreigners."

A man on the street who had already left our bus came back on board and joined the driver. His dress was immaculate and his English was clear and he explained to us in a most pleasant tone that we were not welcome here in Qom. This was a holy city, a place of pilgrimage, and non-Muslims were prohibited. And, he shifted his eyes in my direction, no women either.

Harry dropped his backpack to the floor of the bus and didn't argue with the men. He returned to his seat and I followed him.

"Shiites," Harry said. "These aren't Sunni Arabs. Persians have different rules."

He switched on the overhead light and retrieved our halvah and we laughed about how we'd always dreamed of eating halvah for dinner. We read our books and an eerie silence filled the bus as the smell of stagnant gas fumes returned. I wasn't frightened—there was no reason to think we were in danger—but I couldn't concentrate on my book, either. I was still reading *The Electric Kool-Aid Acid Test* and the Merry Pranksters were driving through Mexico looking for a place to park their bus and party. Hippie life seemed very far away and surprisingly irrelevant. I peered out the window into the shadows of this holy city—quiet and dark, peaceful and inaccessible.

After a time, Harry stuck his finger between the pages of his *Cambridge History* and looked out into the dark.

"We aren't that far from Shushan, you know," he said. "There is a theory that the character of King Ahasuerus might have been based on King Xerxes, the son of Cyrus the Great." Harry kept searching the dark as if he saw something in the distance. "Shushan was near Persepolis, south of Isfahan. I'd really love to go there, but we have to meet Mom and Dad."

The reading light illuminated Harry and he looked like an actor, performing in a spotlight, and I was his audience as he discussed the problematic historical accuracy of the Purim story. I looked at him carefully: He knitted his eyebrows and spoke slowly so that I could follow his words. I loved Harry. More than that, I idolized him—his intelligence, his intensity, his independent spirit. And he cared about me, he reached out for me, even when he didn't have to. Yet in this spotlight now, I could also see that I wasn't very much like him. I wasn't absorbed by the past the way he was, and I didn't really understand history's relevance to the present. Harry suddenly seemed oddly like Mom to me, preoccupied by ideas that had nothing to do with right now. Maybe this was why I stayed quiet so often when I was with them: I had nothing to add that related to their worlds—Harry consumed by the past, Mom obsessed with her future—so I became a devoted listener, a representative of the present in the midst of their distractions.

Harry and I lowered the backs of our chairs and slept peacefully on the bus in the station at Qom. Calls from the minarets woke us up the next morning. We ate more halvah for breakfast and our bus driver brought us some bitter hot tea and a loaf of freshly baked bread. Soon the bus filled with men again and we set down the highway, south, for Isfahan.

It was astonishing. Harry and I waked along beside a long rectangular reflecting pool with a half a dozen spewing fountains and through a garden of manicured fruit trees and a bed of ornamental flowers. This was the entrance to the Shah Abbas Hotel of Isfahan.

Attendants stood at the carved wood entrance and heaved open the mammoth doors for us. Mom and Dad were seated in the lobby bar sharing a drink. They noticed us walk through the inlaid marble lobby and lifted their glasses in a grand welcoming gesture, grinning like newlyweds.

"From bus fumes to Scheherazade!" Harry said to me under his breath.

I didn't say anything about Scheherazade but got the idea that this place was more extravagant than anyone anywhere could imagine. The ceilings were vaulted and lined with tiny bits of mirror in a mosaic pattern so that they reflected colors like a kaleidoscope. The walls were painted with miniature scenes of ancient bucolic paradise—slender women bent over giant flowers in gardens near a lake, men with high hats on horseback holding arrows in their hands. There were Persian carpets scattered on the floors of the lobby. Some of the formal rooms were tiled in aqua and white and others were painted in a soothing combination of mint green and mellow cantaloupe. A circular staircase, carved from rosewood, wound upward by the bar near Mom and Dad.

"This was the shah's summer palace!" Dad told us, gesturing wide with both of his arms. "Not too shabby, huh?"

"Do you kids want to get lunch?" Mom asked. "We've held off eating, waiting for you."

Harry and I looked at each other and burst out laughing. It was only then that I realized how hungry I was after two days of eating only halvah. We sat down for lunch in a lavish dining room and the contrast of atmospheres with our bus ride couldn't have been more striking. Our Cokes arrived in silver champagne buckets. Our rice was tossed with almonds and pistachios and scented with rose water. Harry and I gobbled the food and shared the story of our visit to

Qom with Mom and Dad. They listened attentively and smiled with amusement and my love for my family filled my being—.

After lunch, we strolled by the turquoise-domed Blue Mosque near the hotel and peeked into its courtyard through the white iron gate that cordoned the building off from the street.

"They don't allow you in the mosques if you aren't Muslim," Dad said. "But they don't particularly mind Jews around here, I don't think, as long as they stay to themselves. This new shah, he's even opened up trade relations with Israel."

"It's hard to tell whether Jews are just tolerated or actually admired," Mom said. "But the future is questionable. The young Jews. They don't feel they have a future here. They all want to immigrate to Israel if they get the chance."

The street beside the mosque led to an old shopping district, crowded with antique stores and rug shops and teahouses. But the crowd here was nothing like downtown Tehran's; the tempo was slower and the mood was more somber. Some women wore modern clothes, skirts and eyeliner and earrings, but there were just as many who were draped in black cloth that covered them from their heads to the ground. The women in black exposed their faces but kept their eyes cast to the sidewalk. I walked beside Mom's wheelchair and held on to her arm rail. I found the black garb disturbing. In Afghanistan, the covered-up women wore bright colors that gave them some presence on the street even though their faces were hidden. Here, any mark of personality was erased in blackness and the faces, though exposed, appeared harsh.

In the front window of a store I saw a six-pointed Star of David printed on faded brown paper and framed like a diploma, propped up against the glass. Thick black Hebrew letters were printed below the star. The rest of the display window was crammed with antiques—glasses for tea and table chairs, ornamental knives and old books, carpets and hookahs and decorative boxes.

I tapped Dad on the shoulder and pointed to the star with a questioning look. We exchanged glances but didn't say anything. Strange. We didn't see Stars of David displayed like that in Tehran. Was the Jewish merchant required to identify that way or was the symbol like a form of advertisement, placed there to attract business? Several other stores had the identical sign in the identical place in the shop window. The sign felt welcoming in some way because the Hebrew letters were familiar, but the uniformity of he signs began to make the message clear—this identifier was not voluntary, it was issued to the merchants for display. Not that long ago, in the department stores back in Fort Worth, there were signs identifying "colored" bathrooms and water fountains. Hmm. These Jews here were separated out because they were considered different. I was beginning to understand.

"Dad," I said. "What do you think?"

"I think we need to go into this place and see how business is doing."

An old man was hunched on a stool in the back of the shop and he looked up, expressionless, and didn't speak when we entered his store. The four of us browsed, searching through a jumble of junky-looking stuff stacked in disarray.

"Maybe he has some antique Judaica," Mom said to Dad as she perused the contents of one low table covered with dishes and random knickknacks.

"Excuse me," Mom addressed the man on the stool. She lifted up a pair of brass candlesticks. "Are these candles for Shabbat?"

The man straightened his back a bit and grinned very slightly. "Shabbat. Yes," he said. "Very old. Very special."

He walked over to Mom and began a conversation—cautiously at first—that picked up in tempo and continued over tea at a table behind a curtain in the back of the store. The man had a daughter, as it turned out, who had married just last year and moved to Israel. Oh? You are going there? What a coincidence! Such a small world we live in! Would you please take her this package for me? He handed Mom a shoebox-sized package that was already wrapped in brown butcher paper and tied up tightly with twine. "She needs a tea set," he said and wrote out her address in Hebrew on the paper. And how old is your son? Is he married, if I might ask? I do have another daughter, you know.

We finished tea and bought a pair of carved wooden book-stands from the gentleman. Mom smiled and balanced the shoe box on top of our purchase in her lap.

"Shalom. Shalom," the man said as we left his shop. "Toda. Thank you." He bent over in a slight bow.

"Shalom! Shalom!" the four of us responded. We each smiled warmly.

"He could be an old Jewish merchant anywhere in the world, couldn't he?" Dad said once we returned to the street. "Trying to grind out a living in a tight situation. Trying to look after his kids." I liked the way Dad related so directly to the man. "You got it give it to him, asking for our help. It ain't easy. I'm happy we can give him a hand."

"I don't know," Mom said, lifting the box off her lap and assessing its heft. "This is awfully heavy for a tea set."

"He didn't say it was only a tea set," Harry said. "He said she needed a tea set."

"Sol?" Mom said.

"If we are able to help him out, I'm glad we can do it," Dad said. "What do we care what's inside the box? It's none of our business."

But I cared about the content of the box.

We returned to Tehran on February 23 and learned some shocking news: on February 21, the day we shared tea behind a curtain in the antique store in Isfahan, Swissair Flight 330 exploded in midair as it took off from Zurich en route to Tel Aviv. All passengers and staff on board were killed.

Mom sighed as Dad and Harry and I sank deep into the chairs in the lobby of the Tehran Hilton. We stared together at the gloomy headline of the *International Herald Tribune* that rested on the coffee table in front of us. There was a photograph of the mangled airplane with its Swiss Red Cross tail jutting out of the jumble. We were scheduled to fly from Tehran to Tel Aviv the next morning on El Al, the national airlines of Israel.

"So what do we do now?" I asked, breaking the silence.

"Terrorists," Mom said and she lifted her leg brace to rest her foot on the pedal. "It's despicable. Heartless." The concept of a terrorist was a new to me. I'd never heard the term before.

"What can we do?" Dad said, hopelessly. "Israel is a target. That's the way it is."

Harry lit a cigarette. "It's not like this is the first time. Remember when El Al was hijacked leaving Rome? And then the Athens attack? Frankfurt before that."

"But we're supposed to leave tomorrow, Harry," I said. "And the number of attacks is picking up." I reached for my Turkish coffee. It had turned cold and an oily film formed on the top of the demitasse cup; the grounds had settled like mud on the bottom. "And we are in Iran. How safe can it be?"

"I don't know," Dad said. "I just don't know." He jiggled pistachios in his hand like dice.

"Well, we could try to fly to Cyprus and bypass El Al altogether," Harry said. "Then we could get ourselves to Israel from Cyprus. That has to be a pretty simple route."

A portrait of the shah hung on the wall in a gilded frame near where we were gathered. I looked over Dad's head and stared up at it. His Highness sat erect, shoulders squared and gaze steady, straining, it seemed, to project an aura of order and security, but I wondered. Why was he beginning to look more like a cartoon figure than a ruler to me? The jewels in his annulets were a little too brightly colored. His tight skin, a bit too flawless for a man of his age. Airplanes were blowing up in the sky. What position was he in to do anything about that?

"We could split up," Mom said. She had been unusually quiet since we learned the news about Swissair. "We could fly two at a time." She fidgeted with her wedding ring and her nervous energy reminded me of the way she behaved when we were in India and separated from Dad and Harry on the road to Agra. I knew she was thinking ahead, calculating what she would do if we were attacked. If we were in danger, she couldn't run away like the rest of us could, she was helpless. I knew she felt like a sitting target, like the first one who would be chosen to be terrorized.

"Dad and I could leave first," she continued and her controlled voice quivered. "Then, Jane, you and Harry could follow us the next day. They won't take down two planes in a row from the same city."

"And then what?" Harry asked, standing up. "Then Jane and I can become orphans? Or you get to be childless parents?"

"Maybe you, Jane, would go with me and the men would follow us."

My face hardened. I understood her calculation perfectly: if she died, I would go with her, and if she survived, I would take care of her.

Now I rose up and stood near Harry. This was too much. Mom had crossed a line—we could not split into twos. I didn't argue past history or reason about the future, I just shook my head with defiance befitting Queen Vashti and I said one word.

"*No!*"

I had never spoken so fiercely before, and my force surprised me. I felt the impact of my word. Mom's eyes welled and she lowered her head, isolated-looking in her chair. Dad glanced up from his seat next to where Harry stood. I shifted my focus from one to the other of them. How was it conceivable that we could split up our family? Who among us could be the judge of who would go with whom? None of this made sense. And I was certain of one thing: I was not going to choose between my mother and my brother.

"Okay, okay. Enough," Dad finally said. "No more of this. We are flying as a family on El Al in the morning as planned. If something happens, it happens to all of us together."

Mom took a deep breath: "And what do we do with the tea set from Isfahan? El Al requires that we be at the airport three hours prior to takeoff for a security check. And it specifically says that we should not bring on board any item that we did not pack ourselves."

"Why don't we just leave the package here at the hotel?" I asked.

Dad winked at Mom: "We have nothing to declare."

He looked at me: "The cleaning lady will enjoy her tea."

Then Dad walked over to Harry: "We need to get the hell out of here."

NINE

Tel Aviv, Israel
March 1970

THE SUNSHINE OF TEL AVIV NEVER reached the Hausmans' grocery store on Sirkin Street. Even though our rented apartment shared a courtyard with their shop, our place was sun-filled in the mornings, while the Hausmans' store stayed perpetually dark. When the couple noticed me crossing the courtyard, they slowly looked up, synchronizing the lift of their chins. They sat crouched on the shaded pavement in low plastic chairs reviewing a Yiddish daily. Mr. Hausman folded his newspaper and passed it to his wife. He clapped his hands to his knees and stood, opened the screen door of his grocery. I followed him inside.

"Ach," he gasped as he flicked on the table lamp that sat on his counter. Always *ach*—never *shalom!* never *boker tov!* or any other pleasantness when I came on my daily errand. *Ach.* I didn't like venturing into the gloom of his store any more than he liked the inconvenience of having to attend to me. Boxes of crackers and soup nuts were scattered across the shelves next to cans of sardines and jars of pickled herring. The dairy case was a jumble of wrapped cheeses and cartons of yogurt.

Mr. Hausman sighed, "Nu?"

"Nescafé, please," I said and smiled. I pointed to the label on the empty glass jar that Mom had given me to replace. Mom told me not to be bothered by Mr. Hausman's sullenness. "It's his prerogative to be grumpy," she insisted. "He doesn't mean any harm." She suggested that he understood more English than he let on. "Just show him the jar and be nice," she said. "He deserves some respect."

"Yah. Yah. Farshteyn. Farshteyn." I understand. Mr. Hausman replied to me in Yiddish. He had a stubbly growth of beard but he was dressed neatly in a brown cotton sweater that he tucked into high-waisted trousers in an old-fashioned European style.

He removed a coffee jar from a shelf and tapped it onto the Formica counter at the side of his cash register, its label facing out in case there was any doubt that he had understood my request. He pulled a pencil from a tin can holder and scribbled the cost of the Nescafé onto a stapled pad of scratch paper that was our family's running tabulation. The sleeve of his sweater was pushed up toward his elbow and I saw numbers tattooed on the skin of his inner arm above the wrist. I had never noticed them before: five numbers, unevenly spaced, thick and greenish-black. I glanced away, down at the countertop, and searched for a pattern in the cracks in the Formica.

Mr. Hausman tugged briskly at his sleeve and covered up his numbers before he handed me the Nescafé. The impenetrable expression that had seemed permanent on his face softened slightly. The tension in his jaw loosened as I felt mine tighten. I wished I hadn't seen his tattoo. Why didn't he keep his arm covered? I felt less like a nuisance and more like an intruder now, entering personal territory where I didn't belong and wasn't wanted. I knew so little about the Holocaust. My parents only talked about World War II in whispers and euphemisms: "The Camps." "The Germans." "The Horror." "The Refugees." I didn't have enough information to develop a full impression out of the words I heard, but I received the message not to ask any questions. I understood that the topic of the war was off limits, kept mysterious and hidden on purpose in the same way that our neighbor's diagnosis of cancer was. Don't ask. I knew that Mr. Hausman's numbers were a reminder of something unspeakable.

I paused before I left his grocery store and looked up at the brusque man in the thin brown sweater, curious to know more about him. I wanted to understand what happened, what he had survived, how he had survived it, and why the topic was taboo. I smiled at him again, this time without the residue of sunshine on my face and without a request for assistance. Mr. Hausman considered my smile. It seemed like the first time he ever really looked at me. He muttered something in Yiddish and I didn't respond. He knew I didn't understand him, so he repeated himself in a slower, louder voice. But his words were beyond me.

"Toda," I said in Hebrew and lifted my jar of coffee. "Thank you, Mr. Hausman."

Leah Steinwasser was the only other person I'd ever known who had numbers tattooed on her forearm. She was an artist who had lived in Dallas. Mom befriended her when Leah showed up for services at our synagogue on a Friday night—alone, bewildered, a refugee from Germany. Mom invited her to join us for dinner one evening at our house on Royal Springs when I was six years old.

"Don't stare at the numbers on her arm," Mom warned me as I folded paper napkins into triangles and set them on the table by the side of our dinner plates. "She's from Europe. She's had a very sad life. Very difficult."

I had been around Leah several times before. Mom would call her sometimes and invite her to parties. "It's not good for her to be by herself all the time," Mom would say and lower her head. She and Dad would pick Leah up at her apartment on Walnut Hill and I would curl up in the back seat of the car and watch her double lock her door and then slowly descend the metal stairs of her building while glancing around as if trying to avoid detection. She always looked slightly disoriented—not shy, just vaguely disconnected. My parents would introduce her to their friends and Leah would smile politely and shake hands but not fully engage, even with people who spoke to her in German. It must be because she lived alone, I thought.

I liked to trail behind Leah and watch the manner of her movement. She was quiet and gentle and there was such ease in the way she drifted through a room of strangers, elegant and detached, as if she could dissolve if she wanted to, like a cube of sugar in a cup of tea. She had thick red hair with gold strands shining through, which she pulled tightly to the back of her head in a low ponytail. She didn't wear makeup and the skin on her face was pale and pockmarked, her eyes a luminous gray-green. She only opened her eyelids halfway, which heightened her mystery and enhanced her beauty. I liked to look at her eyes when she wasn't looking at me. Her gaze was fixed and turned inward.

Leah painted a portrait of King David that hung over the piano in our living room between a set of antique Russian zithers. The biblical king wore a tarnished gold crown and held a harp high to his chest at an exaggerated angle. His fingers were thin and tapered and they rested on the instrument over his heart. King David's face was box-shaped and tilted to the side, cast in shadows. He stared into the corner of the canvas as if he were searching the stars in a bleak black sky. But his eyes were hollowed out. King David looked blind.

I counted out the forks, spoons and knives for the dinner table as Mom poured Chianti into the spaghetti sauce that simmered on the stovetop. Our house smelled warm.

"Can Leah speak English?" I asked.

Mom stirred the pot. "She understands a lot. She's smart. She's very creative and sensitive. But she doesn't like to talk too much."

She tapped the wooden spoon onto the side of her cookware. "She's an orphan, Janie. She's got nothing. No one."

I set the forks on top of the napkins, careful that each one was upright and in its proper place. I knew Leah was an orphan. Grandma was an orphan in Europe too. *We were five children. Orphans.* I knew that Mom considered being parentless as the worst fate imaginable. I had a doll called Poor Pitiful Pearl. Her wide eyes spread to the far sides of her face and her dress was tattered and she wore a scarf that covered all her hair and knotted under her chin. Mom had explained that Pearl was pitiful because she didn't have a mother to take care of her. "But when you play with her, it cheers her up!" Mom said when she bought me the doll for Hanukkah. I liked Pearl. I liked her better than my stuffed standard poodle and the other toys that I lined up on the carpet next to my bed. She had a straightforward gaze that was honest, not like my other dolls with pretend smiles and vacant-looking eyes. Pearl may have been piti-ful, but her sadness made her more real. I never felt sorry for her. We kept each other company.

I didn't know about war orphans, though. And when Mom said Leah was an orphan, she didn't mention Hitler or gas chambers or concentration camps. She never said Auschwitz. Why would she have? It's not as if I could have understood what happened there. But I knew there was tremendous misery in the world. And even at age six I understood that what happened in the past lingered and stayed present, even if it wasn't talked about. Things were reminders. Things I could see—Leah's tattoo and Mom's wheelchair and Pearl's tattered clothes, things I couldn't ignore. They were like Grandma's Yiddish accent—remnants that conveyed stories without using words. When I thought about Leah, I sensed that history was inked onto her arm.

"Why doesn't she take the numbers off?" I asked.

"Jane—"

Mom lowered her spoon.

"They don't erase. She can't get rid of them. The numbers are left from her childhood in Europe." Mom flattened her hand over her leg brace to straighten a pleat in her skirt. "They'll never go away," she said.

I finished organizing the dinner table and didn't ask anything more. When the doorbell chimed, I ran from the kitchen to answer it. Leah stood at the threshold in a green sleeveless sundress that matched the color of her eyes. She smiled and I noticed how the expression stopped at her cheeks and only registered slightly in her eyes. When she stepped into the house, I held myself back and fol-lowed behind her. She wore sandals with hard leather soles, but her footsteps didn't make a sound on our tile floor. I followed her, just as quietly and just as light on my bare feet.

"Guten abend," she greeted Mom in German.

"Guten tog," Mom replied in Yiddish.

I climbed onto Mom's lap and listened to the two of them speak foreign languages. Leah had brought some flowers from her garden, and Mom arranged them in a glass vase. Their conversation trailed off into silence.

"Come on," Mom said in English now. "Let's have a drink while we wait for Sol."

Leah pushed the two of us in Mom's wheelchair from the kitchen to the living room. Mom had set out a crystal decanter of sherry, two miniature wine glasses and a box of Winston cigarettes on the marble coffee table near the front window. Evening light angled through the shutters and hit the side of the decanter so that the amber wine glowed. Mom patted the side of my waist as a cue for me to move away, but I wanted to lean back into her chest and lose myself into her body. I wanted to make myself invisible and watch the two of them talk and try to uncover the secret of how they could be friends if they didn't speak the same language. But Mom tapped my waist again and I slid to the floor.

"L'chaim!" the two women said, and they touched the rims of their glasses together.

"To life!" Mom said in English.

Leah pulled two Winstons from the box, placed them parallel between her lips, lit them together, and puffed. She handed one to Mom and the two women sat side by side, sipping wine, pulling drags on their cigarettes, and staring at an unmarked spot in the gray striations of the marble tabletop.

I walked over to the yellow tufted sofa near the piano and sat down facing the portrait of King David. Mom and Leah seemed like lifelong friends, sitting and waiting, lost in their own minds.

Each of them had a story that they didn't want to talk about. And they knew they didn't have to because they understood each other's silence. The cigarette smoke mixed with the smell of spaghetti sauce, and I pulled my legs into my chest and cupped my ankles in my hands. I stared into the hollow eyes of King David, wondering what it was that he couldn't see.

As I left Mr. Hausman's grocery store with Mom's jar of Nescafé, faint memories of Leah Steinwasser returned. I hadn't seen her since that evening of the spaghetti dinner. I never learned what happened to her, why she seemed to disappear, or where that King David painting ended up. Odd. I opened the door to our Tel Aviv apartment and Mom was sitting in the kitchenette, waiting. She was dressed in a plaid Eisenhower jacket and a pencil-pleated skirt and her lipstick was shiny and fresh. The teakettle on the stove whistled at high pitch.

"Janie," she said. "We don't have much time to spare." She drummed her middle finger on the table. "But it's okay. I'm already dressed. My hair appointment is at nine on Dizengoff."

I lifted the kettle from the burner, stirred a cup of Nescafé, and placed the coffee in front of her on our little breakfast table.

"Mom, do I have to go with you to Jerusalem?" I asked.

Mom blew on the surface of her steaming drink.

"It's Golda Meir," she said. "Imagine. She's the prime minister of Israel."

"I know that."

"But don't you understand the significance?"

In fact, I didn't. A friend of Mom's from Dallas, Fanny Schanen, had just arrived in Israel and telephoned our apartment the day before. Fanny invited Mom to join a delegation of women from the

Jewish Federation of Dallas for a private briefing with the prime minister. Could she make it? The way Mom explained the situation to me, Fanny was in a bind. Most of the big-dollar givers in Dallas had canceled out on the trip because of the recent airplane attacks on international flights to Israel. Fanny and Golda were good friends. They knew each other from the 1950s, when they were political activists in the same international Zionist organizations. Fanny didn't want to cancel the meeting with her friend, but she didn't want to arrive at the Knesset with a handful of women and waste the prime minister's valuable time. Rose, won't you and Janie please come join us in Jerusalem?

All I was able to imagine was a logistical mess. Mom had already arranged a driver for the hour-long trip from Tel Aviv to Jerusalem. "It's nothing to get there," she insisted. But I envisioned us circling the parliament building—Mom at heightened nervous attention, me trying to solve the problem of locating a stairless entrance that would accommodate her wheelchair. Once inside, we'd frantically search for Fanny and the ladies from Texas, I imagined. If we found them—questionable—the "meeting" with Golda Meier would consist of some rote stump speech, filled with platitudes about the miracles of the Land of Israel and the need to support it with American dollars. Thanks for the cool invitation, Fanny, but no thanks. I preferred to stay in Tel Aviv, in the tingling sunshine. I'd really rather go to the beach. Or read a book.

I pushed Mom from the apartment through the courtyard and past Mr. and Mrs. Hausman on the way to her hair appointment. The couple was still sitting in the shadows, relaxed in their plastic chairs and reading the news in Yiddish. But this time they looked up energetically and smiled at us, waving good morning as we passed them by.

"Zei gezunt," Mr. Hausman said to Mom. *Go in good health.*

"Gut. Gut," Mom responded, tilting her forehead back toward me. "Taka." *Good. Good. Indeed.*

Mom elicited cheerfulness from the Hausmans that they withheld from most. I knew it was the wheelchair. The wheelchair lent Mom gravitas in their eyes. The Hausmans surely recognized that Mom, too, had suffered through a horrible nightmare. Mom, like them, was a survivor of sorts. She was their emotional equal, someone the Hausmans could greet cheerfully because she shared their depth of experience, their despair.

I squared my shoulders when I pushed Mom through the courtyard. I stepped firmly. Dutifully. Alert and responsible. You see, Mr. and Mrs. Hausman, I am someone of substance too. See my devotion? The responsibility I assume? I figured their assessment of me might improve when they observed the good care I took of my mother. But why did I care what they thought of me? What was it about them that made me want to prove my worth?

A little dog barked on the curb of Sirkin Street. When Mom and I turned out of the courtyard toward Dizengoff, it ran to the side of the wheelchair and nipped at the air near the rotating wheel.

"Gey vek," Mom said and shooed the dog away with her hand. "Go away."

The dog's owner called from across the street and the dog darted away.

"An Israeli dog," Mom laughed. "It understands Yiddish!"

The sidewalk was uneven and the wheelchair rattled as we continued. Bougainvillea bloomed in oversized planters and formed purple-red arches at the entrances of apartment buildings. Some school-aged boys kicked a ball between parked cars to the beat of Israeli pop music blaring from their transistor radios. Curtains fluttered in open windows, and I could smell toast on kitchen tables. In the other cities we visited we were sightseers, confined to taxis and tourist hotels. Here we were residents; we were living in Israel.

"So do you really think we'll get to talk to Golda Meir? Or even get close up to her?"

"It's hard to imagine. She's the prime minister!"

Mom gestured with her hand and I turned the chair onto the sidewalk of tree-lined Dizengoff Street. Café tables were clustered in front of coffee shops. Old men—some in berets, some with yarmulkes—scooted in close around carafes of Turkish coffee, cracked open newspapers, and talked loudly over each other. Street vendors set up orange juice stands and teenagers lined up in their baggy shorts and strappy sandals. Kids bounced by with backpacks. Life! I slowed down in front of a shoe store to check out the espadrilles on the way to Mom's appointment. The owner of the beauty parlor was standing outside an entrance a few doors down.

"Mrs. Sa-ji-nau! Shalom! Shalom!" she called down the sidewalk and approached us with her arms extended. She bent down and kissed Mom's cheek.

"Shalom! I'm Liora," she said to me and wrapped her arm tightly around my shoulder. I stiffened in her grip. Mom and Dad had stopped by the day before to make this hair appointment. I had never met this woman. Why the hug?

Liora must have been in her mid-thirties. She had dyed blond hair that she cut into a pageboy with long straight bangs falling into her eyes and tangling in her dark lashes. Her eyelids were thick with blue powder and lined with shiny black. She was heavyset but wore a miniskirt anyway, with white go-go boots that reached mid-calf. She looked like a caricature of Nancy Sinatra, *these boots are made for walkin'*, already passé back home. If she weren't so big-hearted and welcoming, I would have rolled my eyes and scoffed at her. What was it with these Israelis? If they weren't sour and taciturn like the Hausmans, they were overly expansive and uncomfortably familiar.

I followed Liora into the tiny beauty parlor, maneuvering Mom's chair up and over the front stoop. The place smelled of Aqua Net, just like the shop I took Mom to every Saturday in Dallas. Liora had already rearranged furniture to make room for Mom's wheelchair, removing the black-cushioned chair from the shampoo basin and leaving a spot open in front of the styling mirror. How incredibly thoughtful. Not like me. I made Mom ask me for help. If I volunteered to do much of anything, it was often begrudgingly, with an exaggerated look of boredom. This woman's kindness put me to shame. I dropped down into a visitor's chair at the front of the shop and picked up a rumpled fashion magazine. Go-go boots and bleached-blond hair, how ridiculous. And Liora didn't take care of Mom day in and out like I did, either. I flipped the pages.

"Sweetie," Mom called to me as Liora took hold of her handlebars and turned the wheelchair toward the shampoo basin. "You can come back for me in an hour. I'm in good hands now."

"Bye," I said as I walked away, turning onto the street and merging with the flow on Dizengoff. Clinking coffee cups chimed in the background of mishmashed conversations in Yiddish, Hebrew and German. A passenger bus screeched to a stop on my left and a woman raised her baby's carriage up the front stairs, while an old woman dragged her walking canes out the rear door. I shouldered in with the crowd and lost myself in the commotion, sauntering, my hands dangling at my side, enjoying the freedom of nothing to do. There was a metal chair angled toward a planter with a gnarly ficus tree growing in it. I took a seat and crossed my legs and watched the city parade by.

A man in an open-collared shirt and buckle sandals stopped in front of me and bought a glass of orange juice from a vendor. When he swallowed the neon-colored drink—in one long gulp—I felt the tartness at the back of my throat as if I were taking a sip myself. He returned the glass and spoke to the vendor in a booming voice, laughing, dabbing his forehead with a handkerchief as if he were exhausted from expressing himself so passionately. At first, I thought it was the salty Mediterranean sunshine that made everything in Tel Aviv appear so vivid and immediate. Orange juice was just orange juice, right? What was the urgency about? But it occurred to me that every little thing in Tel Aviv seemed to matter in an exaggerated way. No one was indifferent. Liora was overly friendly. Mr. Hausman was overly dour. The man with his orange juice seemed exuberant over nothing. Emotions weren't veiled.

A man with a long untrimmed beard whooshed by me in the dark suit and white shirt that was the standard of his Hasidic sect. He wrinkled his eyebrows and mumbled into the sidewalk, yet another intense Israeli. I began feeling dull and colorless in this saturated environment.

I thought about Shabbat dinner at Aunt Tilly's. Just a few days before, at dusk, Dad rattled Mom's wheelchair down Sirkin Street, Harry and I trailing behind, as we made our way to a taxi stand on Dizengoff. The sky over Tel Aviv had turned to striking heliotrope—neither purple nor blue, not red or pink or orange. The city glowed and a rare calm had descended on the street. It was Friday, the Sabbath was about to begin.

Tilly wasn't really Mom's aunt, but a first cousin. Mom's father,

Herschel Balofsky, had left Russia as a teenager just prior to World War I, when state-sponsored pogroms were destroying Jewish villages near his Ukrainian home and the czar's army was chasing him down for conscription. Herschel arrived at Ellis Island, changed his name to Harry Blas, and made his way from New York to Detroit. His older sister escaped Russia in the opposite direction and settled in Palestine. Why? Was my grandfather's sister a political activist devoted to the idea of establishing a socialist state for Jews? Or was she religious—unlike her brother—and in search of God in the Holy Land? Nobody knows. That story got lost. But Tilly was that sister's oldest daughter. She was in her mid-fifties now and lived in the ultra-religious neighborhood of Bnei Brak.

Mom transferred into the front of the taxi on Dizengoff and Dad, Harry, and I crammed into the back seat. Mom handed the driver a scrap of paper with Tilly's address written out in Hebrew.

"Do you know where you are going?" the man asked in English. He was young and loose, with long hair and a cocky smile.

"Can you read the Hebrew?" Mom replied.

He drove us across the city to the outskirts of Bnei Brak, pulled over at a traffic light and stopped his car on the side of the road.

"This is as far as I can take you," our driver said as he squinted out his window at the sky. It had turned royal blue now, with whisks of orange curving through it. "Look," he said. "It's getting dark."

He pointed down the street, looking into the distance.

"Just walk straight ahead," he said. "It's close. Don't worry."

We paid him and left the cab, excited to be on our way to meet our relatives.

"Toda," he said. "Shabbat shalom." *Sabbath peace.*

I smiled at him and sensed the sarcasm in his attitude. I liked him! Everyone in Israel felt like family, helpful or not.

The street was empty of cars and filled with a swarm of men heading to synagogue. Each was dressed in the identical black suit, with the same black hat and the same black beard. Each tilted his head toward the sidewalk and clasped his hands behind his back so that it was hard to distinguish among their faces. I couldn't tell the young ones from the old.

"You know, technically it's not dark," Mom said. "He could have driven us a little closer, I think." She looked down into the flowering potted plant that she had selected for her aunt and was balancing on her lap.

Dad wheeled the chair against the flow of men, and Harry and I walked close to Mom's side. We could just as well have entered a village in eighteenth-century Poland. Stern expressions were set on the men's faces as they rushed by. I tugged at the hem of my miniskirt and pulled the white clingy blouse away from my chest.

"Mom, there aren't any women here," I said, reaching for the rail of her chair.

"They're making dinner," she said and looked at me sideways. "While the men pray."

Two men approached Dad on the street. They had broken away from the crowd and were circling their hands in front of their chests with exaggerated gestures, talking loudly in Yiddish. Harry and I grinned and rolled our eyes. It was impossible to tell if they were agreeing or arguing with each other. We thought maybe they were playing a joke on us. But these men weren't laughing. They stood too close to Dad and now they yelled and waved their hands in front of his face.

Dad angled Mom's chair way from them. "Gey vek," he said. *Go away.* Mom waved her hand in the air and the men moved on, clucking their tongues and shaking their heads.

"What was that about?" I asked.

"It's just one more block," Mom said. She lifted the plant from her lap and held it tightly in front of her chest.

I felt a thump. I didn't see anything when the stone was thrown, but I heard the clang on the side of Mom's wheel and it reverberated like a thud in my chest. Dad stopped pushing Mom and squatted down to inspect the spokes of her wheel. I looked over at Harry, who was rushing across the street to a man standing alone on a curb flicking his hands in the air and shouting, "Shabbos! Shabbos! Gey vek!"

"She can't walk!" Harry yelled at him. "It's my mother! She can't walk! Do you understand?"

I took the plant from Mom and grabbed her hand. It felt dry and cold. Dad darted us to the opposite side of the road.

"Shabbat Shalom," Harry said when he jogged back over to join us. He looked disgusted. "Since when is a wheelchair a breach of Shabbat?"

"Can we just go back?" I asked. "Do we have to go to Aunt Tilly's? We've gone this long without knowing her."

But Aunt Tilly was expecting us.

She cried when she opened her door to greet us. Aunt Tilly bent over to kiss Mom, "Oy. Oy. Oy." She squeezed my face between her hands, "Shayna maidelah." *Pretty girl.* She babbled in Yiddish and her breath smelled nervous. Aunt Tilly was short and her posture was sturdy and self-confident. Her floral-print dress hung loosely toward her ankles and swung as she welcomed us into her house. The lights were dim and there was an odor of boiled meat. The dining room table, covered with a white cloth and set for ten people, occupied the entire space of the book-lined living room. Two candlesticks glowed next to a challah on a TV table, friendly and familiar, but not familiar enough to overcome the strangeness I felt. Tilly was the one person in Israel who was actually kin, yet she seemed more foreign than anyone I had encountered here.

Tilly seated Mom and Dad and me on one side of the table across from her son and daughter-in-law and granddaughter. She pulled out the chair at the head of the table and ushered Harry there across from her husband, who hadn't lifted his head from the book he was studying. No one in the family spoke English except for the granddaughter, who was painfully shy. I pinched the palm of my hand with my fingernails and forced my tongue against the roof of my mouth in order to suppress laughter that seemed ready to arise out of nowhere. I didn't know what struck me as so funny. I just knew that I was out of place.

When the door closed behind us after dinner and we were back outside on the street, my laughter found focus: "How was that fish head?" I asked Harry. "Yummy! Yummy!" I rubbed circles at my belly and a tear dropped down my cheek from laughing so hard.

Aunt Tilly had prepared gefilte fish for dinner—patties of ground carp mixed with matzo meal, garnished with boiled carrots. I passed on the dish because I was now a vegetarian. But Harry was served a double portion with an added delicacy on his plate: the boiled head of the carp! Tilly ceremoniously offered this symbol of fertility to the twenty-two-year-old visiting bachelor from America. "Essen! Essen!" she exclaimed. *Eat!* The fish head was cut below the gills and its eyes were glassy and blank, its skin shiny yellow. I watched Harry pluck flesh from the bony head with a fork and wash down each bite with a swig of Coca-Cola from a shot glass. My rebellious brother, so proud of his nonconformity, grinned and ate dutifully as the rest of the family watched. I'd never seen Harry behave with such acquiescence; complicity was always my job. He looked ridiculous behaving in the exact manner that was expected of him.

Walking away from Tilly's house, Harry's gait trailed to a creep and I glanced at the side of his face. His skin had the same yellow tinge as the carp he just consumed.

"Yummy," I said, licking my lips and continuing my taunt. "That must have been one delicious fish head!" It was hard to catch my breath I was laughing so hard. Harry, the rebel, turned good boy. I, the good girl, turned mocking.

Harry put his hand on his chest and burped. Then he turned toward the curb and heaved. On this quiet Shabbat street in Bnei Brak, Harry purged himself of Tilly's delicacy and emptied his gut of her abundant goodwill. My stomach was fine, but my mind churned. That quiet granddaughter at the table, I kept thinking, that could have been me if my grandfather Herschel had escaped Russia for Israel instead of New York. And my mother might have been the one busying herself preparing a fish head for the Sabbath. But would she have? Or would she have rebelled? And would she have never contracted polio? A gurgle rose from my stomach, and I suppressed it with a full breath of Tel Aviv's night air.

Mom and I made the journey to Jerusalem. She was right. The trip from Tel Aviv was an easy one, and it took us just under an hour. A young Israeli soldier with an Uzi submachine gun slung over her shoulder stood guard at the Knesset's entry gate and greeted us with a casual "Shalom" as she shepherded us inside the complex. The building was new, less than five years old, and its contemporary design made wheelchair access simple. I glided Mom's chair over the marble floors, and we wound through walls of Jerusalem stone until we got to the Hall of State. Marc Chagall's massive tapestries hung there: his recent gift to Israel's new seat of government.

"For God's sake," Mom sighed. "No wonder the art world's abuzz."

I sat down next to her on a wooden bench and faced the triptych of tapestries that draped from the ceiling to the floor of the two-story atrium. Each section was crammed with colorful imagery—Moses grasping tablets, a lone lion floating, villages on fire, angels spreading their wings, Jacob on a ladder, candlesticks aflame, men and women in dance circles.

"A tapestry of this size is unheard of today," Mom said. "Marc Chagall isn't a religious man, you know. But here he's returned to biblical themes." She looked over at me. "People do that."

People do? What people do? We were a Jewish American family. We lit candles on Friday nights and shared a family meal. Usually we went to services. On Sunday mornings we'd eat bagels if we could get them, and laugh at rabbi jokes while we listened to Allan Sherman records. Of course, we celebrated the holidays and I was a bat mitzvah. We were Jews! But I had no sense of what my parents actually believed. We didn't discuss religion, we acted on it. And we rarely talked about the Bible. People return to biblical themes. You have to know something and leave it before you can return.

I circled my eyes over the tapestries but couldn't find a place to focus among the floating images swirling in patchworks of color, unlinked and disconnected. It reminded me of all the places we had visited: the veiled women in Kabul and the injured child on the road to Agra, Tehran's crown jewels and Mr. Hausman's tattooed numbers. How did those random images relate? Would I ever stitch them coherently together? I glanced away from the artwork to clear my head, looked through the atrium and out the window to the sky.

When I looked back, King David floated in front of me in a robe the color of maraschino cherries. King David, like the portrait that hung above our piano on Royal Springs. But this King David's eyes were iridescent blue and his beard was lime Jell-O green. His body stretched like a lion's at the edge of the tapestry, and his bare feet dangled in the air. He clutched a harp at his chest and gazed out at the chaos swirling in the tapestry about him—red angels and blue angels, Moses beckoning with his tablets, a candelabra burning at his feet. David hovered beside the fray, his crown balanced on his head.

"King David," I said to Mom. "Chagall went in big for King David."

Mom looked up at him and nodded. "A complex character," she said. She kept her eye on his crown and began a monologue about King David with details I never imagined she knew. A fierce warrior, she explained, and also a poet. With his political sophistication he united the warring tribes of Israel, but he fought with his family and made enemies. He was brutal and he was repentant. He sought out girlfriends and slayed giants and played the harp at night in the breeze by an open window. "Human," she said. "Flawed like a Shakespearean hero." She corrected herself. "More like a modern antihero. He was conflicted. He suffered with his power." Now she was the one who looked out through the atrium at the sky. "He's a real study in leadership."

"Yeah," I said. "I don't know."

But I liked the orange flush of David's cheeks and the comprehending look of his wide forehead. And I liked the way he kept aloof, remaining to the side of the whirling commotion. He appeared both sad and satisfied. I tilted my head and aligned it with the King's. I wished I could jump up and float beside him, like the light-footed bride behind his shoulder and the mysterious fiddler balancing upside down near his feet.

"Rose Saginaw!" Fanny Schanen's voice boomed through the Hall of State and stirred me from my fantasy. "I should have guessed you'd beat us here!"

Fanny bent over with a grand gesture to kiss the air beside Mom's face. I stood up to greet her and Fanny dropped her hands onto my shoulders. "Thank you for bringing your mother today." She looked at me directly. "I'm so glad you could join us." You're so dutiful, I heard her thinking, and I returned to my job as the deliverer of Mom.

Mom introduced me to the other women in the Dallas contingent. There were seven in total, and each was dressed Jackie Kennedy style in a knit suit with polished pumps and hair sprayed into a bouffant.

"This is my daughter, Janie." Mom beamed and I nodded hello to everyone. I wondered about the wisdom of the psychedelic Peter Max scarf in my hair. It had more in common with Chagall's colorful characters than it did with the women in this group. But, anyway, who cared what I wore?

Fanny clasped her hands at her chin and wrung them in excitement. "Let's go, ladies."

I looked back over my shoulder to the floating King David. But Mom beckoned and I grabbed her handlebars.

Golda Meir entered the conference room through a wide-swinging hinged door, unannounced and unaccompanied. Our group had been seated just moments before. The eight of us stood the instant she appeared, and Mom straightened her spine and leaned forward in her chair. Golda paused and nodded as the door swung to a standstill. "Shalom," she said without a smile. "Welcome to Israel."

Golda was as plain-looking and unassuming as anyone I could imagine. Her steps were firm and her shoulders sagged. Her wiry hair was twisted into a bun, and her skin had a thick and rubbery coarseness. This grandmotherly figure in a beige knit suit, white graduated beads, and orthopedic shoes was the leader of the State of Israel?

She jiggled her hands at the wrists. "Sit. Sit," she said. "No formalities here. Please, sit down." Her voice was husky, and her accent was Midwestern American. She pulled a chair from around the oval conference table. Golda's chair was cloth-covered and low-backed like the rest of ours, but a pad of paper and ballpoint pen were set out for her, along with a pitcher of water, a silver ashtray, and a box of Winstons with a book of matches. The table was made from polished blond wood and in the middle of it was a mound of oranges balanced in a glass bowl. Golda took her seat and we followed her lead. I studied the prime minister across the table— her brows arched high over pale blue eyes, the lids were heavily hooded, and her thin lips seemed parched.

"I'm glad you've come," she said. "Thank you." She took a cigarette from the box and tapped it on the table. It was a tap I interpreted as impatience. "It's not easy. I know."

Golda felt familiar from the moment she entered the room. It was only six months earlier that I had seen her picture on the cover of *Time.* Mom had set a copy of the magazine on the marble coffee table in our living room in Dallas. I came home from school, dumped my backpack onto the couch, and slumped down next to it. Mom was aglow. She grabbed the magazine and pulled it tautly between her hands. "Jane! You've got to see this!" She grinned into Golda's likeness. "Israel has elected a woman prime minister, and here she is on the cover of *Time*." Mom handed me the magazine and I looked at Golda. Her expression was solemn. She looked worried and old, gazing over her shoulder, her neck thick and wrinkled, no makeup and no smile. She seemed simple and powerful, unlike any woman I had ever known. And yet she was so understandable. I recognized something in her direct gaze and the rounded creases on her forehead. "She reminds me of Grandma," I said and handed the magazine back to Mom.

"She's one of the most powerful women in the world," Mom replied. "Imagine that."

But I didn't imagine anything. I didn't spend any time thinking about Golda Meir until the possibility of this meeting in Jerusalem came up, when all I could picture was the hassle involved in trying to see her. But now, sitting across the table from the prime minister, I was intrigued. How could this old woman be such a mighty world leader? Where did her confidence come from? Why did I feel so immediately comfortable in her presence? I leaned back in my chair and considered the balanced oranges in their glass bowl. What was the source of Golda's power?

"You were scheduled to be a large group from Dallas. What, forty women?" Golda asked, scanning the room without moving her head.

Fanny Schanen stood to speak. "Madam Prime Minister," she addressed her friend. "People are afraid to fly."

Golda winced and Fanny dropped her head.

When she looked up again, Fanny clasped her hands at her waist. She was broad shouldered like Golda. And she, too, was plainspoken. "I don't need to tell you, Golda, the PLO and these hijackings—this recent Swissair attack—it takes a toll. Our women had to make tough decisions. They have families."

"Sit, Fanny," Golda said. "Sit down."

"We can't give in, you know that," Golda continued. She struck a match and lit the cigarette she had been holding between her thumb and forefinger and stared into the flame before blowing it out. "There isn't any choice for us. And we can't afford pessimism. That's not an option."

Golda drew down on her cigarette, holding it in one hand, and hammered the knuckles of her other hand onto the table. The beat was firm and deliberate. I felt the vibration in the wood in front of me, as if Golda was knocking on my door, trying to wake me from a nap, from my teenage stupor.

I leaned into the table as Golda continued talking. She delivered a short homily about the marvels of Israel: the Jaffa oranges blooming in the Negev, the survivors of Auschwitz opening shops in Tel Aviv, the hard-fought battles for existence. Everything a miracle in its own right, she insisted. But nothing was easy.

"We are building a modern country out of nothing. What are we? A little country of refugees. In a desert. No water. No oil either, I might add. A little oil wouldn't hurt, you know." She chuckled as if she was telling herself an old joke. The wrinkles on her brow shifted around. "We're in a bad neighborhood, don't forget." She looked at me. "Our young people bear a heavy burden."

Golda was silent.

"We've fought enough wars," she went on and I felt the disgust in her voice. "We don't want any more victories."

I searched the wall behind Golda for a place to divert my attention. I was thirteen in the summer of 1967, just two years earlier, when Israel triumphed over Egypt, Jordan, and Syria in the Six-Day War. My parents watched the *CBS Evening News* with Walter Cronkite each night and reacted as if the air battles were in Texas and the Israeli soldiers were our next-door neighbors. Mom welled up and Dad swore under his breath and I watched the coverage along with them and thought that the war looked like a movie. But now the Palestine Liberation Organization was attacking Israel-bound airplanes in Europe and bombs were exploding in the Jerusalem markets. Hints of a new war were rumbling. I was older now and the battlegrounds were closer. I began to sense the responsibility that weighed down Golda's shoulders. Would she be answerable for another war?

"We pay a price," Golda said. "Our youngsters do."

Golda picked up a pen and scrawled some notes on her pad. She jotted down a few words, paused, underlined something, paused again, scribbled and underlined once more. Her hand was heavy. Her power was immense. Her mind was elsewhere. Yet she chose to sit down at this table with us?

"So," Golda said. "What else?" She slapped down her pen and raised her eyebrows.

The woman beside me stood up. "Madam Prime Minister," she said. "What can we do in Dallas to help you?"

Golda folded her arms and leaned both elbows onto the table. She looked amused and slightly playful. "I'll tell you exactly what you can do," she said. "Send us your children for a summer. Our young people are isolated."

She smiled at me as if we were old friends. It was an insider's smile, an unmasked communication saying *you know what I mean.* I wondered how she saw me: a dutiful daughter? an earnest

American? Did she by chance catch a glimmer of herself in my tight-skinned youthfulness, just as I had recognized myself in the shadow from the weight of her eyelids?

"Let your kids come learn Hebrew. They can work on a kibbutz. It might toughen them up and do them some good! They'll swim in the Mediterranean Sea and have some fun. Eat falafel. Maybe they'll fall in love."

I must have wiggled in my seat when she mentioned love. Golda gestured toward me with her chin, "How old are you, darling?"

"Fifteen," I answered and squeezed the knot on my Peter Max.

"Come back and stay for a while, won't you?" she asked and held my gaze.

I had a sensation that this whole meeting, Golda's whole message, was directed at me. I knew that it wasn't so. I wasn't as self-centered as that. And I understood that Golda was a politician, skilled in her rhetoric. But I felt then that she genuinely cared about me. She saw me. Not as just as an extension of Mom, brought along to push her chair, and not only as an add-on to Fanny Schanen's group from Dallas. Golda was building toward a future, and she saw that I had one in front of me. I had independent worth in her eyes.

"Well," Golda drummed her fingers on the tabletop. "Enough," she said. "It's enough, already, for today." She smiled. "My son is coming for dinner, and I need to make something for him to eat."

Golda pushed back from the table. She stood and walked out the door, shoulders rounded forward and head erect. Silence hung behind her, complex stillness that no one dared disturb. The door swung closed and Golda drifted away, as spry on her feet and heavy in her heart as Chagall's King David.

TEN

Istanbul, Turkey
March 24–25, 1970

I SLOWED DOWN MY STEPS OUTSIDE the eastern gate of the Grand Bazaar of Istanbul. Mom and Dad were eager to shop in the massive indoor market. Of course they were. Weren't they always excited about shopping? But I wanted to linger in the narrow streets that wound along the outskirts of the bazaar and poke around near the cafés and food stalls in this old section of the city. I was interested in watching the old men in the alleyways on their low stools, drinking tea from glasses next to their gurgling water pipes. The smoke from the hookahs rose slowly and smelled sweet. But I had no one to wander with. Dad avoided the bumpy cobblestone streets because they dented the rims of Mom's wheels, and Harry had left the family for a weeklong trip to Africa. He departed Israel for Kenya and Tanzania a few days before we left there for Turkey. I knew if Harry were here in Istanbul, he would have asked me to go with him to search for old coins. We would explore the side streets and Harry would explain, "Istanbul has been a trade center since before the Byzantine period…" I would gladly have tagged along beside him, thrilled for the invitation, keeping pace with his long stride.

But I trailed, instead, behind Mom and Dad through the open stone gate and into the hubbub of Turkish commerce. The corridors of the bazaar were jammed with stalls pushed up against each other, under what looked like an optical illusion of an infinity roof. Men yelled out from behind their merchandise—carpets, brass trays, dried figs, hookahs, leather handbags, glassy blue beads to ward off the evil eye, Turkish delight dusted in powdered sugar. "Come look, miss!" a man cried out as I passed by. "Mademoiselle?" another smiled and held out a sample of whatever he sold. "Habla Español, señorita?" It was whipped-up commotion inside that ancient marketplace. But the smell of coffee mixed with leather and wool muted the tumult somehow; and the high curve of the ceiling created a feeling of expanding space. Stained-glass lanterns cast a butterscotch tint and I felt comfortable, surprisingly drawn in, and welcomed.

Dad pushed Mom over the smooth tiled floor to a booth stacked up with Turkish kilims. The flat-woven carpets were folded into piles like blankets and reached the height of the handlebars on Mom's wheelchair. Each carpet's geometrical pattern was woven differently, and the colors were variations of dusty blue and earthy oranges and greens so that the shop gave the impression of being one large patchwork quilt.

Mom reached for a top carpet and flipped it over to examine a different one toward the middle of the pile. She and Dad had learned a few tricks of the carpet trade in Tehran. They understood, for starters, that carpets on the top of a heap were set out for tourists—readily available for a quick sale to undiscerning customers. The better pieces, without fail, were hidden and out of reach. They required a hunt, and an investment of time.

Mom checked the underside of one of the tribal rugs and tugged on a knotted string that hung loose and dangled. "Quite coarse," she said to Dad when he leaned in over her shoulder. "Loosely woven."

"D'hairst?" Dad said in Yiddish, keeping his gaze fixed on the carpet but gesturing with his head toward the shopkeeper that was approaching.

Mom flipped to another rug. "Taka," she whispered. "Imported blue."

And Dad nodded knowingly.

This was all code. Mom and Dad's banter sent encrypted information. I knew the setup. The more blasé they appeared, the more engrossed they were; and the less hurried the pace of their words, the more excited their actual interest. But I never understood the nuances beyond that. It was hard for me to tell, for example, when their interest in making a purchase dissolved into pure amusement with the art of a hunt, a pleasant way of passing time together. Shopping was recreation for them, like playing cards or Ping-Pong.

More like dancing, really. In the summers, when Mom and Dad set out on road trips in a pursuit of visiting every state in America, they made a habit of stopping at antique shops along the way. I remembered the summer a few years earlier when we were driving through Virginia on the way to Washington, DC. I was holed up in the back seat of the car behind Mom's wheelchair when I heard the familiar conversation begin:

"Sol," Mom said pointing to a roadside billboard. "There's an antique shop at the next exit; let's see what they've got."

"It's got to be good shaving mug territory around here," Dad answered, flipping the blinker to exit. "Maybe we'll find a tobacco grower." Dad had a collection of over a hundred antique shaving mugs. He displayed his favorites—occupational mugs—in a cabinet at home that a neighbor in Fort Worth had built. He owned hand-painted mugs decorated with the emblems of early American trades: butchers' tools, firemen's badges, tailors' sewing machines, locksmiths' keys.

I pushed open the screen door to the Victorian house in Virginia and the hardwood floors creaked as Dad rolled Mom's wheels over the threshold and into the narrow aisles of the shop. Mom and Dad began their hunt and I dropped onto the needlepointed seat of a Queen Anne chair.

Mom leaned over the edge of a dining room table and turned over a china plate that she held up to the light. "Wedgwood," she said, tapping it with her fingernail.

Dad found a set of oversized keys and jiggled them in his hand, evaluating the weight. "Lead," he said, shaking his head in astonishment.

I sighed loudly to demonstrate my boredom. The only thing astonishing to me was that my parents found such fascination in this old stuff.

Dad cleared his throat and reached to the top shelf of a hutch where he found a shaving mug hidden amongst a set of pressed-glass stemware. He inspected it closely.

"Baby," he said, and his eyes lit up. "A policeman! There's a whistle and a bobby. See what you think."

Mom took the mug and checked the markings on the bottom. "English," she said, nodding slight approval.

When the shop owner approached to see if she could answer any questions, my parents remained quiet.

"Just browsing," Mom finally said, dismissively.

My parents hardly wanted help. They knew exactly what they were in the market for and the last thing they wanted was to reveal the object of their quest. As soon as the woman left the room, Mom looked up at Dad and said, "See what she's asking for the mug. It's rare. We don't have a policeman."

He returned the mug to its place on the shelf and Mom raised a second Wedgwood plate to the light. It was almost like music was playing and they were moving to its beat. They tapped and touched and ran their fingers over the surface of objects in complete harmony of purpose. They sent each other side glances and nodded and shrugged as if they were flirting on a dance floor.

"Can we go now?" I asked.

Dad ignored me and reached back for the shaving mug. He left the room and returned minutes later with a wide grin and the mug wrapped up in newspaper.

"Thirty bucks," he said to Mom. "There's a chip on the rim near the handle."

Mom glared up at him, as Dad bowed and placed the mug on her lap.

Would that same dance continue in this carpet stall in Istanbul?

I was so tired of rug shops. In Iran, we had spent hours shopping for carpets. I sat atop mounds of Persian rugs and drank sweet tea while Mom and Dad haggled over Sarouks and Kashans. I traced my fingers over the shapes of flowers and songbirds, growing drowsy, as they arranged shipments of carpets back to Dallas.

"I'm going to go exploring," I said to Dad, who was still leaning over Mom's shoulder and admiring a Turkish kilim. "I'll be back."

"Stay close by where we can see you," Mom instructed. "Stay close," she repeated as I walked away.

Yet more code from Mom. "Stay close by" meant *Go on. You can leave. But stay safe and out of trouble.* It was Mom's way of granting me freedom to roam while struggling with her inability to watch over me. It's one of her earliest instructions.

When I was in preschool and Harry was in the fifth grade, Mom would take a nap after we dropped my brother off at Walnut Hill Elementary. One morning we drove from the school to Dallas Fair Park instead of heading home for her rest. Mom angled the white '57 Ford under a tree near a giant pond where swans and ducks swam in the spray of a fountain. She rolled down her window and I snuggled up next her to watch the birds.

"Be kind to your web-footed friends." Mom sang after a while. "For a duck could be somebody's mother."

When I looked up, she tucked her fists deep into her armpits and raised her elbows like wings. "Quack! Quack!" she said and flapped her arms, laughing. Her gusto was rambunctious. Was Mom mocking herself? Did she think of herself as a web-footed duck? Her attitude felt out of place in the peace and tranquility of the park. I didn't laugh along but looked away from her instead, to the quiet ducks that glided on a swell of water. How fun it looked, coasting on a calm surface like that, undisturbed.

"You can feed the ducks," Mom said as she unlatched the glove compartment and handed me a plastic bag of Mrs. Baird's bread. "But you need to stay close by."

Mom clicked open her leg brace and shifted her hips, slowly and laboriously, underneath the steering wheel, forcing her back into arch. "I need to be able to see you," she said.

I took the bag of bread and closed the car door behind me as Mom lowered her head to the back of the car seat and let her eyes drift closed.

A tuft of pampas grass sprouted near the edge of the water, and I nestled in under the curve of its plumes. I could hear Mom's gentle snoring through her open window and the wind blew ripples across the top of the water. I slid off my Keds and pulled my legs into a crisscross. The ducks bobbed blissfully near the shore, and I lost my thoughts in the serenity of the park.

Then a large swan appeared and honked at the ducks in front of me. A second swan joined in and nipped the first one at the back of its neck. The two swans wrestled—heads entwined, wings flapping, water splashing everywhere. I watched the drama from my perch, surprised and amused by the commotion.

"Janie!" Mom yelled from the car. "Quick! Come back!"

I twisted around and Mom was clenching the rim of the steering wheel.

"The swans are playing!" I said.

"Swans bite! It's not safe!"

I pushed my arm into Mom's in the front seat of the car just as the swans settled down and began drifting away. Quiet returned to the pond but Mom was still agitated.

"Things change very quickly," she said. "You have to be alert. Careful."

Mom's breathing was labored, and I rested my head on her shoulder, trying to calm her.

"We know another song about swans, don't we?" she asked after a while and began to sing:

There once was an ugly duckling
With feathers all shaggy and brown

I leaned away from her as she went on:

QUACK! QUACK! Get out!
QUACK! QUACK! Get out of town.

I hated that Danny Kaye song, even then. The ugly duckling was shunned by the others and forced out of town but grew up on its own and returned one day as a magnificent swan, the most beautiful of all the birds. I knew there was a lesson embedded in that song about the way life changes and how what was once one way turns into the opposite; an ugly duck becomes a swan, the loser wins. But the song made me uneasy because it seemed that Mom thought she was as an ugly duckling. I thought she felt badly because she couldn't watch over me. I thought she felt that she should be shunned. I didn't want my mother to think of herself as a duck. I just wanted her to be calm.

Years had passed since I thought about the Ugly Duckling song, but now, in Istanbul, when I heard Mom's instruction to "stay close by," I felt the pull inside of her that wanted to release me but still felt insecure about not watching me closely enough. I walked past the brass trays and coffee pots, ignoring the salesmen calling out for my attention. But when I entered a section of the market filled with leather goods, my interest was stirred. Belts hung in storefronts like light curtains. Wallets and purses, suitcases and cushion covers were stacked onto tables in front of the shops. I stopped in the middle of an aisle to observe. The leather was yellowish and undyed, the texture looked stiff and uncured. The styling of the purses was out of date—box-shaped satchels with molded leather handles when the fashion now was shoulder straps. But the smell was enticing, like the earthy aroma of the Texas stockyards. I lingered at one of the storefronts and fingered a wallet.

"Welcome," an old man said in a deep Turkish accent. "Look. Please. Take your time."

He was seated on a wooden stool by the doorway of his shop. He wore a white shirt, billowy dark pants, and felt shoes that turned up at the toes. His hair was graying and his manner was soft, nothing like those young men selling brass trays who had called out *Hello! Good price! Special for you!* Those overeager men were easy to shun. This man was calm. He pulled in a long drag on the mouthpiece of his hookah and the water in his pipe gurgled at his side. He looked as if he wanted to smile.

I studied his merchandise without uttering a word. The belts were too flimsy and the pillow covers were useless. The wallets were rough to my touch. I started to turn away and wander farther down the aisle when I noticed a carry bag, the size of a small suitcase, in the back of the shop hanging high from a hook. It was yellow-beige and the shape of a half oval, with two pockets on the front and a long skinny belt that wrapped around the middle over the top zipper. I hadn't noticed another one like it in the bazaar and it was the only one this man had on display.

I pointed up at the bag and looked at the old man.

"Française?" he asked.

I smiled demurely.

"Italiano?"

The man narrowed his eyes when he handed me the bag. He seemed intrigued by my origins. My silence had become a mystique.

"It's good quality," he said, returning to English. "The leather is from a camel."

I ran my hand along the bag's surface. There was a patina to the leather, a soft glow. The bag had authenticity, character, as if it was old and had been used before. Yet when I unzipped the top, the inside was pristine and stuffed with balls of loosely wadded newspaper. I pushed the paper aside and felt the bumpy texture of the unlined cavity. I'd never seen anything like it.

But I didn't have any liras and I had never bargained for anything before. Dad always gave me money if I wanted food or a Coke. And Mom took me shopping; Harry to the movies.

"Thank you," I said, smiling broadly as I revealed my English.

He smiled too and tossed back his head. "American!" he said. "I knew it!"

"Yes."

"I'll make you a good price."

"I don't have any money."

"Fifty Turkish liras."

"Twenty," I said and held my fingers in a *V*.

He handed me the bag: "Forty liras."

I returned it: "Twenty five."

We felt the dance! I gave into the swaying rhythm, and we twirled circles around the price for this camel-leather bag. Our steps were firm, yet nimble. But still I had no money, and I couldn't make a deal. I lowered my head and took a step backward.

I didn't expect to find my parents behind me in the aisle.

"What do you have here?" Dad asked.

I pointed to the bag and summarized the negotiations over price. Dad cocked a smile to the side of his face, and I could read in it his amusement.

"Go on and see what he'll do," Dad urged, and if he winked at the old man, I didn't see it.

I stepped forward again. "Thirty-five liras," I said. "But no more."

"Forty is my last price."

We settled at thirty-five Turkish liras and Dad paid the bill. The salesman handed me the bag and offered me a leather coaster for free. I didn't know whether I got a good deal even then, but I knew the experience was invaluable. I entered a new world where I held my own in the marketplace. What else could I do now? Where else might I glide with new confidence?

"She could be Turkish," the old man said to my father.

I blushed and stayed quiet.

We returned to our hotel for dinner that evening and before dessert was served, Dad excused himself from the table and went up to our room alone.

"His color isn't good," Mom said, pursing her lips. "I'm worried."

Dad was pacing the carpet when Mom and I joined him. Sweat dripped from his chin and he was holding his waist, doubled over in pain. It was a kidney stone, he was certain. He hadn't had one in a while, but he recognized all the symptoms.

At two o'clock that morning, Mom called the front desk for a doctor. If the stone wasn't passed by noon, the Turkish doctor warned, Dad would need to have surgery at the hospital down the street.

I sat on the corner of the couch near Mom and we held hands as we watched Dad pace. The sun began to rise over the Bosporus and the black sky turned smoky orange. Now I crossed my arms over my stomach, feeling queasy.

"The saints go marching two-by-two. Ba-room! Ba-room!" Mom began to sing. She fisted her hand and swung it in front of her chest like the leader of a marching band. I knew the song was a diversion for her, a show of determined and optimistic energy, but it didn't play well with me in my tired and diminished state. Mom and her songs. Will it ever end?

"Please don't sing that now, Mom," I said. "I can't take it."

Mom laughed nervously and Dad drank his seventh glass of water. Then he turned from us and disappeared into the bathroom. I heard him howl before he flushed the toilet.

"Look here," he said, returning to the room where Mom and I sat waiting. He flattened out the palm of his hand and in the center of it was a jagged pebble, the size of a tiny diamond.

"We passed it!" Mom said, clenching her fists.

Dad shot me a quizzical expression. We? But I just looked out the window at the intensifying morning sky.

"Yes, we did," Dad said to Mom. "Now what are we going to do?"

ELEVEN

Aboard *The Apollo*, Greece
March 26–31, 1970

A NEON-TO-NAVY CONTINUUM FORMED the sky-to-seascape of the Aegean Sea, gradations of heavenly blue for as far as I could see to the barely discernable horizon. Dad wheeled Mom down the rope-lined entrance ramp of *The Apollo* cruise ship and I followed behind them, swinging my camel-leather bag at my side.

It was the maiden voyage of *The Apollo*, its inaugural three-night cruise though the islands of Kos, Delos, Rhodes, Mykonos, and Santorini. The men and women of the crew were lined up military style in their nautical uniforms as we boarded with a throng of other passengers. The crew members appeared to be nervous—one struggled to contain her laughter, another checked the brass buttons on his navy blazer as if he had never worn such a garment before. When I returned a smile to an attendant close by, he stiffened and turned his glance immediately away, adjusting the brim of his captain's hat.

A steward located Mom and Dad and me in the middle of the crowd and strode across the deck. The aura of his authority preceded him: his hat stood inches higher on his brow and the gold trim at the cuffs of his blazer was more pronounced than that of the rest of the crew. He clutched a clipboard at his chest and, when he reached us, he stood for a moment at attention. Then he bent toward Mom and began speaking in broken English. *Please, it is no problem, I promise, madam,* he began. He had arranged for a very special room. Very special. It seemed, he went on to apologize, that the ship had some initial difficulties—the elevators were not yet operating, nor was the air conditioner in service. But the telephone system, he assured us, was almost in ready order.

Mom straightened her back and searched over her shoulder for Dad, who was still standing behind her. "Well," she said, straining to make eye contact with him. "Our maiden isn't quite ready, is she?"

Dad tightened his grip on Mom's handlebars and his face reddened.

"Apollo, my rear end—," Dad said to the man with the clipboard. "The Son of Zeus the All Powerful," he added sarcastically.

I reddened too. Not because of the condition of the ship, but because I feared Dad was about to start yelling the way he sometimes did when he got overwhelmed by wheelchair logistics. I didn't want him to unleash his frustration on this man and take off with unstoppable force. I felt sorry for Dad with his bursts of rage over situations that were out of his control. Too often he lashed out at salesclerks, orderlies, waiters, or car-parking attendants as if they somehow bore responsibility for Mom's blocked access. So many times, I'd heard him bully a bewildered bellman unloading our luggage in the lobby of a hotel: *And how the hell do you expect me to get my wife up that flight of stairs?* As if the poor man could remedy the situation; as if anyone could. I'd cringe with embarrassment and Mom would stiffen when Dad became abusive like that. Mom would lower her pitch and whisper in a controlled voice: *Sol, it's not his fault. There's nothing he can do.* But this time she intervened before Dad had a chance to get riled up.

"Sir," Mom said to the Greek steward. "I am not able to walk, you see." She raised her hand to her eyebrow in a vague salute, squinting up at him, before she continued in her disarming manner: "Will I be able to continue on this voyage?"

Mom spent the days of *The Apollo* cruise in the upgraded suite that the apologetic man with the clipboard arranged for us. No shore leave for her. She read books about ancient mythology while Dad and I traversed the islands by foot and on the backs of mules. Dad and I returned in the afternoons with souvenirs from our excursions—white stones from the donkey trails of Kos, a bottle of ouzo from a café on Rhodes, a pink-flowering branch picked from a tree in Santorini. Mom sniffed the air around us and insisted that she could smell the pack animals on our clothes. If she felt the least bit slighted by her confinement to the room, she never let it be known. In fact, I sometimes felt that we intruded on her coveted solitude when we returned to the cabin at the end of a day. She would look up and shove a marker between the pages of her book, but her smile looked distant, her attention elsewhere.

For the first two evenings of the cruise, Mom and Dad and I joined the other passengers at an evening buffet in the dining room down the hall from our cabin: seafood and champagne, ice cream and baklava and tiny wild strawberries. Most of the tourists were Greek nationals and our dinner conversation focused on the story of our American vice president, Spiro T. Agnew. Our Greek American vice president, who was the son of an immigrant from the island of Chios. In America anything was possible, no? Look at the spaceship America just landed on the moon—the *Apollo*! Greek too! Ha, ha! Like this cruise ship! How funny! And we learned from our fellow Greek passengers that extravagant party preparations were underway for our last night at sea. A grand gala was in the making—belly dancers and live Greek music, fancy flaming desserts and fireworks—on the top deck, under the stars!

On the top deck. Hmm. Mom didn't say a word as the party arrangements were discussed. But she did book a salon appointment. I thought that most likely Dad would arrange for extra crew members to help lift Mom up the staircase. The evening of the party arrived, and I dressed up in my pale yellow cardigan and black miniskirt, tied the Peter Max scarf into my hair, and joined my parents in their cabin.

Mom's back was to the door when I entered, and I couldn't see her face. She had wheeled over to the side vanity and was concentrating on the application of her makeup. I walked over to her side and put my hand on the arm of her chair, but Mom didn't look up. She stretched the corner of her eye out to the side and glided an eyeliner brush over the top of its lid. Her hand shook and she drew the line a second time.

"Baby," Dad said from across the cabin. "It's not the first time and it won't be the last." He took his sport coat off a hanger in the closet and slipped it on. He paused for a moment and stared down at his shoes. "Baby," he said again and walked over beside me, standing behind Mom and rubbing the back of her neck. "We'll have fun. Come on. Let's go." But Mom blinked nervously into her mirror and still didn't glance up.

I felt the tightness of Mom's stomach in my own and walked away to leave my parents together. I knew, without them saying anything in front of me, that they had argued. I imagined Mom had urged Dad to leave her in the cabin and go to the party with me. "Live it up! Dance! Have a good time, I'm fine," she probably told him, swearing that she was perfectly happy in the room by herself. Then Dad most likely insisted, as he usually did, that he would not go without her—he would either stay back in the cabin or lift her up the stairwell to the upper deck. I knew how Mom and Dad behaved: each one wanted to accommodate the other. Neither of them would yield. And both wanted to shield me from their discord, as if I couldn't read meaning into their irregular silences.

Mom finally snapped her tube of lipstick closed.

"Okay," she said. "Let's go."

Dad and I positioned Mom's wheelchair between us at the bottom of a metal stairwell. The flight was steep and narrow and the lighting above the stairs was dim—this was a back stairwell, not really meant for tourists, a more private and hidden one. Mom bent over and raised the flaps of her foot pedals as I stabilized her chair with her handlebars. When she straightened up, Dad leaned over and Mom raised her arms toward him. She took a deep breath and grabbed the back of Dad's neck as he scooped her out of her wheelchair. He caught his balance. I pulled the chair away and collapsed the wheels together. This was the easy part.

I remained at the foot of the stairs as Dad began the ascent. Step, pause. Step, pause. He was in good physical shape, and he was slow and deliberate in his climb—step and pause, step and pause—but Mom was a heavy load to carry. I watched intently, hoping my close attention lent him strength. *Don't fall, Dad.* Mom's legs waved at his side. Her braced leg hung lower than the other one and it looked so heavy and limp. It wasn't often that I saw Mom from afar and out of her wheelchair. I felt exactly the way her leg looked—reinforced and strong on the outside, slack and helpless within. I couldn't see Mom's face, but I imagined her stoicism as she stared at the ceiling as Dad climbed the stairs.

Step, pause. Step, pause. I remembered the same halting cadence from a time when I was nine years old. It was *click, pause, click, pause* back then when I also viewed Mom out of her wheelchair, and at a distance from behind. I was sitting on the floor of our house on Sarita Drive, the summer after third grade, watching *The Jetsons* on TV. The space-age family zoomed through the cosmos in a silver capsule, with no seatbelts or helmets. I was distracted by the labored clicking sound down the hallway, just outside my parents' bedroom. *Click, pause. Click, pause.* Mom and Dad had recently returned from their yearly visit to Warm Springs and Dr. Bennett had prescribed a set of crutches for Mom to practice on. He ordered her to walk with them for fifteen minutes a day, an experiment to see how she could do. Mom had showed me the crutches when she unpacked from the trip to Warm Springs. "I don't know what good these crutches could possibly do me now," she told me then. She asked me to balance them behind her skirts in the back of her bedroom closet.

The sound persisted. *Click, pause. Click. Click, pause. Click.* I turned away from the Jetsons and toward the uneven rhythm. What I saw was more alien than the flying spacecraft on TV: Mom was out of her wheelchair, upright and struggling over the new pair of crutches. I had never seen her walk before. Look how tall she was and how broad her hips were, spread out wide like the seat of her wheelchair. Look at her stiff back, flat with no curve, rigidly held in place by the metal of her corset. She may as well have been flying with the Jetsons, the sight of her walking was so completely unnatural. And at the door of her bedroom, abandoned, she had parked her empty wheelchair.

My spine tightened at the sight of her struggle down the hall. *Click, pause. Click, pause.* She looked so ill at ease. Mom's hips and shoulders didn't line up. Her back jutted behind her at an exaggerated angle and her shoulders pushed into her neck from the pressure of the crutches under her arms. Her full pleated skirt hung like a flag, covering the top of her leg brace, while the spring coil and the lever at the side of her knee hinge were visible at her hemline, pathetically mechanical. Her steel brace—that began at the top of her thigh and lined the sides of her leg until it connected to her orthopedic shoe—looked thicker and more awkward somehow. This view of her body from a distance, misaligned and encased in steel, was agonizing to behold. She was broken and weighed down with equipment; she was a stranger to me, uncomfortable and unsure of herself. *Don't fall* was all I could think. *Don't fall, Mom. Don't fall apart. What if I can't pick you back up?*

I was relieved I couldn't see Mom's face. I didn't know if she was proud or pained by her broken gait and I didn't know how she wanted me to feel either. She looked so jumbled up, but did she know how crooked her alignment was? Her skirt waved loosely as she lifted a crutch and secured its rubber tip inches in front of her—maybe that soft sway felt graceful to her. Maybe there was freedom in the lilt, and she enjoyed the coolness of air circulating through her legs. She swung her braced leg out to the side until it lined up with her hip, or her shoulder, or the metal of the crutch. I couldn't tell what she was trying to do or which body part she was aiming to align with. I was so glad that Mom couldn't see me. She would be able to tell by my tight face that I didn't want her to walk.

I wished she would return to her empty wheelchair, where I knew she was safe and in control of herself. Her movement was smooth and predictable when she sat in her chair. And I knew exactly where to stand, how to push her, when to pull and when to push. In her seat, on top of those sturdy spoked wheels, I understood her strength—and her uncertainty and her fragility too.

Please don't fall, Mom.

Step, pause. Step, pause. Dad was almost at the top of the metal staircase when I climbed up behind him with Mom's empty wheelchair. I spread the wheels apart, opening up her seat, and I set the chair's brakes in place and held the handlebars steady as he lowered her into her chair. Well done, Dad. He drew a handkerchief from his pocket and wiped his hair back from his forehead. Mom adjusted her leg brace and straightened some wrinkles from her skirt. There was no other recognition of the effort involved in the ordeal of the ascent. I pushed open the door to the top deck of the ship and the three of us rushed toward the music of the band. Opa!

Flares and sparkles shot high into the night sky and reflected off the water in silver ripples. Blinking lights on distant islands blurred to combine with stars in their constellations. Another firework exploded behind me. I looked up in awe, at the center of our expanding planet.

Dad pushed Mom into the middle of the crowd of mingling tourists. All the tension about the arrangements of her arrival was released into the beat of the music and the explosion of fireworks. Passengers lined up to greet Mom, shaking her hand and kissing her cheek, welcoming her to the festivities. Mom grinned her glamorous best, red lips sparkling. And when a belly dancer sauntered over to her, veils whirling and finger bells chiming, Mom laughed and shimmied her shoulders right back. She slid a bill under the bikini string at the performer's hip. The partiers broke into applause—not for the dancer's flair, but for Mom's.

Clap. Clap. This must be exactly what Mom remembered when she told me about the clapping tourists on their hotel balconies in Jamaica. It was 1948 when Mom and Dad took that trip. Harry was a year old, and I wasn't yet born. Mom had just returned home to Detroit after three months of polio rehabilitation in Warm Springs, Georgia. I was about ten years old when I first heard the tale, but she repeated the story often.

"We were still newlyweds," Mom always began. "We stayed at Tower Island on the beach." She arched her eyebrows as if she could catch the ocean breeze and described the fuchsia bougainvillea in a glass vase and the bowl of tropical fruit that awaited them in their bedroom. They slept with a sliding door opened to the beating of the ocean waves. And the staff wore starched white uniforms and served them frozen daiquiris on paper doilies.

"A valet was assigned to us," Mom said. "One morning after breakfast your father took me to the beach. He scooped me out of my wheelchair and lifted me high into the air! Then he walked me into the water. Our valet instructed me to hold onto his muscular shoulders and he swam far out into the ocean, pulling me behind him on his back. Sol stood on the shore in his swimming trunks, grinning and waving, his blue eyes sparkling."

I always loved hearing that part of the story because I could envision it so clearly. The ocean water must have been invigorating and I could imagine the freedom Mom felt out in the waves without the weight of her heavy equipment. And Dad! How thrilled he must have been to see Mom happy after those long months in Warm

Springs. It was easy for me to envision him standing in the sunshine, like some sort of movie star, his expanding chest and glowing smile.

"That night your father and I played Ping-Pong," Mom went on, abruptly changing her tone. She spoke more slowly now: "All the hotel guests stood on their balconies and watched us. They cheered for us and clapped."

Mom paused here, allowing the drama of the situation to set in. I had never seen Mom play Ping-Pong before, but I imagined she was good-natured about it. Dad probably served her easy balls, and she must have returned one or two. Mom said that the valet walked up to her privately after the game.

"Missus," Mom told me he said. "Everybody thinks you're so great, playing Ping-Pong like that from your wheelchair. They clap and carry on, but I've been watching you. You're not so great. Mister picks up all those balls you miss and keeps the game going. That's why you look so good."

Mom ended the story there, without any explanation.

What was I meant to make of that story? It baffled me each time Mom repeated it. *I've been watching you. You're not so great.* I thought the valet was mean-spirited to say that. Why did Mom retell a story that belittled her ability and so blatantly undercut her dignity? Maybe the whole story was really about Dad. She built Dad up into the role of a strong mythic hero who lifted her from her wheelchair with his mighty arms, grinned benevolently from the shores of the sea, and made her a champion in the eyes of the public. Clearly, to the other tourists, Mom was a star because she wheeled herself up to the table and engaged in a game of table tennis. But what did Mom think about herself? Did she agree with her Jamaican valet that she really wasn't all that great? Or did she think she was as terrific as those tourists on their balconies did?

Up until that party on the top deck of *The Apollo*, I had decided that the Jamaican story was like the story of the Ugly Duckling. Both of those stories turned on the same ironic twists. Mom was like the Ugly Duckling, taunted and jeered but in the end the grandest of them all. So the joke was on the Jamaican valet, who, like the mean ducks in the pond, didn't have the foresight to recognize her great potential. If the Ping-Pong story is about the magnificent woman that Mom would one day become, then it made perfect sense that she retold it because she was confident in the person she was now. My mother was the beautiful swan! But this figuring on my part didn't answer all the questions. Because then, what about Dad-the-hero, who lifted her into the air and smiled at the shore of the ocean? Where was the irony in his role?

I stood on the top deck of *The Apollo* and watched Mom flash a smile and bask in the attention of the Greek passengers. A breeze blew the scarf away from the back of my neck and a shiver lowered down my spine. I thought about the Jamaican Ping-Pong game, and I realized how profoundly right the valet was: Dad made Mom look great. The Jamaican story took on new mystery when I realized there was no irony to it. I glanced at Dad. He posed behind Mom's wheelchair holding a mixed drink in one hand and resting the other on her shoulder. He was laughing too, greeting the other passengers right along with Mom. That Jamaican story was heartbreakingly honest. Dad lifted Mom up a flight of dimly lit and hidden stairs so that she could enjoy herself at a party, because he loved her. Her happiness and his happiness were completely intertwined. Yes, it was a story about dependence, but not just physical dependence. The Ping-Pong story was about the back-and-forth forces of love. A perplexing kind of love that remained hidden—like a backway stairwell.

TWELVE

Belgrade, Yugoslavia
March 31–April 2, 1970

DR. KADELBURG LIFTED ONTO THE TOES of his spectators and reached to the top shelf of a bookcase in his Belgrade office. I couldn't see his face, but I had the clear sense that he was smiling to himself. He seemed like such a contented man, alert and soft-shouldered. He grabbed a copy of the Sarajevo Haggadah and walked over to his desk, where he set the book next to his electric typewriter. His chair creaked when he sat down. The Haggadah's creamy white sleeve was protected with cellophane: *Haggadah* in Roman font and golden Hebrew letters; *Sarajevo* under it in smaller black script. Dr. Kadelburg's windowless office was lined with books, but the others were larger and uniform in size, dark brown and leather-bound.

Dr. Lavoslav Kadelburg was president of the Federation of Jewish Communities of the Federative People's Republic of Yugoslavia. He was a sixty-year-old retired officer of the Royal Yugoslav Army. The Nazis had held him prisoner during World War II. Now he was a judge, a legal scholar, and a close associate of President Marshal Tito, the first and presiding president of this socialist people's republic.

When Mom first mentioned that we were going to Dr. Kadelburg's office, I had imagined a medical man. She and I sat in the lobby of the Metropol Hotel while Dad went out on the street to hail a taxi. I asked Mom why were we going to the doctor. Was everything okay?

"No, no," Mom said. "Dr. Kadelburg is a doctor of philosophy. A PhD."

"What kind of philosophy?" I asked.

"He's a legal philosopher," Mom said. Bernard Levy, the president of the Jewish Federation of Dallas, had given her the doctor's contact information. Mom said we would get an inside perspective on life in a socialist country: "An interesting glimpse behind the Iron Curtain."

Mom spoke the words dramatically, as if we were entering an ominous, forbidden place. But Belgrade seemed pleasant enough to me with its broad boulevards and sidewalk cafés. Maybe it was a little drab, but so what? I liked the Old World feel of the city—subtle and serious, not glitzy like the Greek cruise ship.

"Who knows if Sol will have any luck locating a cab," Mom continued. "It's a socialist country, you know. No free enterprise." She tapped her fingernail on the metal siding of her wheelchair and shifted her focus, darting her eyes through the hotel lobby.

Mom was too distracted for conversation, so I scanned the lobby hoping to find Harry. I was curious about this Iron Curtain. The meaning of the term wasn't clear to me at all. Was the curtain physical? Had we crossed some barrier? Harry could explain it. He had just returned from a week in Africa and rejoined us in Athens the day before we flew to Yugoslavia. He met up with us at the Athens Hilton in his torn Levi's, with his canvas backpack slung over his shoulder, his eyes puffy. He fell asleep early that evening, still in his blue jeans.

"Was Africa cool?" I asked him the next morning from my seat across the aisle from his on the JAT flight to Belgrade. While Harry was away, I realized how much I missed him and his ramblings. It occurred to me that I listened to my brother the same way that I listened to Bob Dylan lyrics back home. I didn't care that much about the specific words either of them spoke—I connected more to their emotion. When I nodded my head and mouthed the words along with Dylan to "Subterranean Homesick Blues," I knew I missed most of his references: *You don't need a weatherman to know which way the wind blows.* But I knew that his thoughts were complex, even though I didn't understand them. And with Harry: I lost track of the dates and dynasties and revolutions he talked about, but it didn't matter. His intensity was more interesting than the events he focused on. When Harry wrinkled his brows, I wrinkled mine; when he smirked, so did I. Dylan and Harry were both zealous characters. Neither of them was satisfied with things as they were. They were restless in ways that I wasn't. Part of the mystique, I realized, was that I couldn't quite identify what it was that they were rebelling against.

"I wasn't a tourist in Africa," Harry answered me on the flight to Belgrade. "It wasn't like that. I didn't go to Nairobi to sightsee." He flipped the pages of his *Cambridge History* and created a rustle that was louder than it needed to be. I didn't ask another question. Harry had experiences that he'd never fully share. Fine. I didn't need to know everything he did. I wiggled a JAT airsickness bag from the magazine holder in front of my seat and slipped it into my carry-on to add to the pish bag collection Mom and I were amassing. I opened my paperback and read until I dozed off.

By early afternoon we had checked into the Metropol Hotel in central Belgrade. An art deco chandelier clung high on the lobby ceiling and a marble floor covered the wide-open expanse. The moment I stepped into the cavernous space, I was taken back by the hotel's stripped-down ambiance. There weren't paintings on the walls or carpets at the front desk. The mossy-colored velvet furniture, dull and utilitarian, was sparingly arranged, more like an office lobby than a hospitality center. Unusual. Great effort must have been taken to avoid any feeling of luxury.

But despite the muted decor, the hotel was teeming with activity. Men in dark suits and thin black ties paced the lobby floor—dozens of them—rubbing their clean-shaven faces, lost in concentration. The sound of clicking heels echoed off the bare walls. The USSR vs. The Rest of the World chess tournament was underway. Bobby Fischer, the American chess prodigy, had checked into the Metropol days before. Harry explained that Bobby Fischer was a chess grandmaster, as famous around the world as Mick Jagger, he insisted. Chess? "It's all about strategy," Harry said. "You're looking at nerves of steel in this room." Bobby Fischer was matched against the Soviet champion, Tigran Petrosian, and their set was scheduled for the next day on the mezzanine in the Metropol's grand ballroom. Now Harry was pacing the floor in his Adidas, rubbing his chin through his beard, and bobbing his head.

"Communist versus capitalist in a socialist country," Harry said. "The front line of the Cold War. Right here, right now."

Harry knew all the facts of Bobby Fischer's life. Fischer started playing chess at the age of six in Chicago. Fischer was a certified genius. Fischer was considered the greatest living chess player in the world, and he was only twenty-seven. Fischer's game was open to the public, so Harry decided to stay back at the hotel while we visited Dr. Kadelburg. When I tried to find Harry in the lobby before our appointment, he was nowhere to be found. So I never did get a Cold War primer, or a lesson on the Iron Curtain, before we set off for the doctor's office.

Now Mom and Dad and I sat opposite Dr. Kadelburg at his desk. The thoughtful man raised his fingertips to his fleshy lips and peered at us. His eyes were calm and cloudy blue and their lower lids drooped. He had a high forehead and a generous smile and his white shirt, open at the collar, gave him an approachable appearance. But despite his likeable demeanor, his presence was weighty and solemn. I could imagine him in dark robes behind a high court bench. I could imagine those seeking justice nervously anticipating his judgment.

"We Jews have lived in Yugoslavia since the Roman times of the first century," he said when he finally spoke. His voice was deep and his English accent was Oxford impeccable. My body softened and my attention heightened in the authority of his presence. I leaned in toward him. "Yet we lost eighty-seven percent of our community in the war. Over sixty thousand lives. Murdered by the Nazis." He squared the corner of the Haggadah on his desk and folded his hands on top of it. "This month will be twenty-nine years since the Fascists invaded Belgrade. April 12, 1941. I was down the street here," he motioned with his chin toward his bookcases. "At my parents' home." When he paused, he didn't need to explain the fate of his parents; it was abundantly clear in the sideways glance, his eyes downcast and unfocused, that his parents were included in the murder statistics. "Now," he said, looking up at us. "Those of us lucky enough to stay alive—and we *freely* choose to stay here—are part of a socialist experiment. We are believers, you might say, in a social idealism."

Each word Dr. Kadelburg spoke was flawlessly formed, but I knew I missed a good part of their meaning. I wished Harry had come along. He might have inquired about this social idealism; he might have questioned the doctor about the extent of freedom in Yugoslavia. I knew about communism from duck-and-cover drills in elementary school. At the sound of a siren, I would drop my notebook and crouch under my desk, covering my neck with my palms. I knew about Khrushchev and Castro, more or less. And the Vietnam War—that was about communism also, about the Soviet Union and the domino effect. But socialism wasn't communism, and Yugoslavia wasn't the USSR. I knew that too.

"There's no Iron Curtain here in Yugoslavia," Dr. Kadelburg said, focusing his attention on me. "We keep good relations with the Soviets and with the West. We aren't communists, you do understand," he spoke as if he read the uncertainty in my face. "If we choose to leave Yugoslavia, we are free. We go." He flicked his hand in the air and smiled.

Dr. Kadelburg appeared guileless, like an earnest teacher with a lesson plan. I listened, the A+ student on the front row who strained to understand but let others ask her questions.

"Where do people go if they leave?" Mom asked.

"Israel, mostly," Dr. Kadelburg said. "People go to search for family. Survivors mostly, from the camps," he said. "From the war." He checked his watch and covered it with the cuff of his shirt. "We are free now."

I knew he was entering murky territory. Free to go to Israel, okay. But what about other places? And what about people who weren't Jewish? Were they free to leave? Dr. Kadelburg's charm was appealing, but it couldn't cover over the impression that there were gaps in what he was telling us. I kept thinking about the Iron Curtain. Where, exactly, was it?

"I'd like to show you this book," Dr. Kadelburg said. He slid the Sarajevo Haggadah over his desktop in my direction. "This is very, very interesting, I think."

Dr. Kadelburg explained that this Passover Haggadah was a reproduction of one of the oldest illustrated Hebrew manuscripts known anywhere in the world. Its survival had an astonishing history. The original book was printed on parchment in Barcelona in 1350. It was smuggled out during the Spanish Inquisition of 1492, when the Jews were expelled from the Iberian Peninsula and their libraries were burned to the ground. How it reached Sarajevo, nobody really knows. But in 1888 it was sold by a Bosnian Jew named Cohen to the National Museum in Sarajevo, and it was protected there as a treasure of the Austrian Empire. Then, after Hitler invaded Yugoslavia in 1941, a Nazi officer stormed the museum and demanded possession of the Haggadah. How did the book survive this time? Again, nobody knows for certain, but many believe the museum's curator slipped the book out a window and had it smuggled to a Muslim village, where it was hidden under the floorboards of a mosque. "This book is a symbol of our survival," Dr. Kadelburg smiled broadly. "Go on," he said. "Take a look inside."

I opened the book to its frontispiece:

THIS IS A LIMITED EDITION OF THREE HUNDRED
COPIES, PUBLISHED ON THE OCCASION
OF THE FOUR HUNDRETH ANNIVERSARY
OF THE ARRIVAL OF THE JEWS TO BOSNIA AND
HERZEGOVINA. SARAJEVO, OCTOBER 1966.

The reproduction was printed on thick glossy pages and the Hebrew script was bold and elaborate. Songbirds and flowers and mythical beasts embellished the calligraphy and intertwined with the text in cobalt and coral, copper and gold. Castles. Warriors. Women in flowing gowns holding goblets to their chests. This Haggadah looked more like a book of fairy tales than the black-and-white paperback edition that we read from at our house on Passover. But when I thumbed through the pages of the Sarajevo version, I recognized the text.

"Here are the Four Questions!" I said and looked up at my parents, astonished. I pointed to the illuminated page and began reading the Hebrew: "Mah nish tana ha lailah hazeh."

It was easy to recite the questions. I had posed them every Passover since I was six years old. Each spring, Dad led us through the Haggadah, the story of the biblical exodus. We sang in Hebrew at our seders, made a mess with crumpled matzo, and celebrated the liberation from Pharaoh's bondage in Egypt. "Once we were slaves, now we are free," Dad would read and lift a glass of wine and say a blessing. Then he'd call on me: "Janie, now it's your turn. Ask the Four Questions." I'd stand beside my folding chair and perform, chanting Hebrew, then reciting in English: *Why is this night different from all other nights? On all other nights we eat either bread or matzos, why on this night do we eat only matzos? On all other nights we eat all kinds of herbs, why on this night do we especially eat bitter herbs? On all other nights we do not dip our herbs in condiment, why on this night do we dip our herbs twice? On all other nights we eat either sitting or reclining, why do we recline on this night?* I had memorized the questions and delivered them with confidence, but I never really listened to the answers. The questions weren't mine, somebody else wrote them for me to recite.

But now I was curious and questions flooded my head. Freedom. How do you know when you are free? I handed the Haggadah back to Dr. Kadelburg and asked him, "Do you use this Haggadah today?"

Dr. Kadelburg didn't answer. Instead, he opened his desk drawer and removed another book that he placed next to the Haggadah. This book was slender and bound in black linen. After a moment, he picked it up and handed it to Mom, watching her carefully as she read the gold letters embossed on the front: *The Crimes of the Fascist Occupants and Their Collaborators against Jews in Yugoslavia, Belgrade (1957).*

Mom weighed the book between her hands, raising and lowering it slowly. She inspected the cover and ran her fingers over its gold lettering, and then she pressed her lips together and held the judge's gaze as she returned the volume to him, unopened.

"I see," she said. "It is hard to be a believer."

Dr. Kadelburg slid the black book underneath the Haggadah.

"We Yugoslavs are not religious people anymore," he said and he blinked rapidly. "We don't celebrate the holidays too often. But we remain a very close Jewish community. President Tito protects us as an ethnic minority."

He glanced at me: "We believe in the socialist state."

He looked at my parents: "For the moment."

He looked at the two books and shrugged.

Nobody spoke for a while. The buzzing sound from a fluorescent light on the ceiling seemed to get louder and I rubbed my ear. I didn't need any explanation in order to understand that Dr. Kadelburg maneuvered well in areas of ambiguity. I wondered though: Was he forbidden from celebrating Passover like the Jews in the Soviet Union? Or had he lost interest in religion since the

Holocaust? Was it maybe a little of both that kept him from celebrating the holidays? It was impossible to tell from his cryptic
responses. I smiled at the astute old man. He looked at me as if
evaluating the quality of my attention and I didn't divert my eyes.

"I suppose the survival of this Haggadah is a miracle of sorts,"
he said, sliding a pointed finger over the cellophane protection.
"Even for those of us who don't believe in such things."

A miracle, even for those who don't believe in such things. He wasn't
trying to be humorous; it seemed more that he was amused by the
limitations of his own way of thinking. I felt on the edge of learn-
ing something of consequence from this man. The Iron Curtain
and the survival of the Sarajevo Haggadah and the closed book
of war atrocities—those images blurred together and made vague
sense to me. What was it? What unspoken lesson was I grasping to
understand? I glanced at the two books stacked on Dr. Kadelburg's
desk. I knew about another place with two versions of history:
one a triumphant saga that was repeated yearly and celebrated like
Passover, and the other a dark and inaccessible story, left closed
like that book of war atrocities. And the mythic Iron Curtain—that
barrier that couldn't be crossed—I had a sense of it as well. I had
been to Warm Springs, Georgia, with Mom the year before and my
memory of that complicated place returned. Warm Springs was
another land of guarded hope and hidden catastrophe. Another
place that was veiled behind a curtain.

Every year in the spring after Passover, Mom traveled to Warm
Springs for an annual physical examination. And every year before
she left, she would sit beside me, widen her eyes, and raise the pitch
of her voice, as if starting to tell me a fairy tale. I heard storybook
accounts of the world-renowned rehabilitation center in Georgia

that President Franklin Delano Roosevelt established in the 1920s for polio patients. "Warm Springs is more like a *resort*, really, than a hospital," Mom liked to say. She told me about the Little White House that FDR built, nestled among the pine trees, and I heard about dignitaries and royalty who traveled there for visits. The president had a girlfriend at Warm Springs, she never failed to remind me: "He was *very* human." On Thanksgiving Day Roosevelt hosted a feast. He carved a roasted turkey, delivered a homily, and then leaned against the entrance to Georgia Hall and shook the hand of every polio patient he hosted. "At Warm Springs, the most important thing we gained was a lesson in self-confidence," she'd say. "FDR set a hopeful tone, and we polios left rehab knowing we could accomplish anything we set out to do." But Mom was silent when it came to the actual care she received there. And when the time came for her yearly visit, she ordered a bottle of tiny red pills from the pharmacy and began popping them days before she packed her suitcase. Dad would rest a hand on her shoulder, "Come on, baby, chin up." I'd stay home with a housekeeper, and Mom and Dad would return from Warm Springs a couple of days later with lifted spirits along with an adjusted wheelchair and leg brace, fresh new corsets, and several boxes of new orthopedic shoes.

In early April of 1969, just weeks before my fifteenth birthday and months before we set out on our trip, Mom asked me to take her for her annual physical. "I'd like to show you Warm Springs. I think it's important," was all I remember she said. I was surprised she invited me. Fairy tales aside, Warm Springs had remained a mystery because of the way my parents carefully omitted details of Mom's visits. I was curious, but cautious, about polio. I'd never known anyone else with the illness or anyone else in a wheelchair.

Polio was something Americans didn't get anymore. The Salk vaccine was a miracle of modern medicine. No more fear of paralysis. No more iron lungs. No more crippled children with leg braces.

"Sure," I shrugged. "When do you want to go?"

Days later, Mom and I flew to Atlanta. A minivan with *Georgia Warm Springs Foundation* stenciled onto its side waited for us near a taxi stand. A driver in a chauffeur's cap hollered "Welcome!" when he noticed us and slid open the side of his van. He released the valve on a hydraulic lift and, with a puff, a platform lowered from the vehicle to the street. I had never seen a van retrofitted for a wheelchair. How would I ever stabilize Mom's chair? Her nerves? How would I manage to maneuver her chair onto that mechanical contraption? I gripped Mom's handlebars and pushed her closer to the lift.

"Let me do that." The chauffeur smiled.

"It's lovely today, isn't it?" Mom said as she handed me her purse and nodded to the man.

The driver and I traded places. He reached for Mom's chair, and I stepped backward onto the curb. When he tipped her front wheels up and lowered them onto the floor of the lift, I recognized his familiarity with the task in his fluid, confident movements. He rolled her to the center of the platform and stooped to fasten her wheels onto the metal base.

"Yes, ma'am," our driver said. "A fine day."

I watched Mom levitate. She crossed her hands on her lap and her shoulders hung loosely from her neck as she gazed into middle space and the platform slowly raised her into the air. She didn't gesture nervously or call out last-minute instructions: "Janie. Stand here beside me. Stabilize the chair with your hand, will you?" She didn't check her brakes or even clench her jaw. Instead, there was a liberating charge in the empty space that surrounded her, an aura of composure. Something gently lifted in me too when I realized that Mom had trusted her wheelchair to the hands of a stranger.

The driver steered Mom's chair inside the van and secured it to the floor with a chunky metal chain as I scooted by her to the back-bench. It was an hour's drive to Warm Springs, and we were silent for most of the ride. Why was Mom so quiet? I matched my gaze to hers and watched the white stripes pass in a soothing rhythm down the center of the highway. She had turned still and inward, a rare and calming demeanor. Inward and silent, I knew that this was how I generally appeared. I was the one who so often stared into space while Mom grasped and grabbed at her equipment, directing and instructing everyone in her proximity. I was the teenager who shielded myself in an armor of stillness as a way of asserting inde-pendence and separating from Mom and her never-ending needs. *I sat in my bedroom listening to the Beatles on headphones. I gazed out the car window on the Dallas–Fort Worth turnpike and imag-ined tadpoles darting beneath the surface of a swamp.* But now Mom was the self-contained one. She pulled herself into a world of her own and pushed me away with her silence. We were entering new territory.

I glanced out the window to the side of the highway at the bloom-ing dogwoods. Clusters of white flowers flickered in the sunshine. They weighed the boughs down like clumps of snow and the reflec-tion off the blossoms was so intense that I had to look away. I messed with the hair at the nape of my neck and examined the cracked vinyl on the backrest of Mom's wheelchair. It had never occurred to me that I could have stayed at home. That I could have said no and let Dad accompany her as usual. Mom must have thought long and hard about asking me to come here. I never asked her why.

Our driver flicked on his blinker, and we exited Roosevelt Highway onto an unpaved road that curved up a hill. Mom adjusted her posture and tapped her polished fingernail onto the van's windowpane.

"President Roosevelt loved that red Georgia soil," she said with the fairy-tale lilt that signaled our approach to Warm Springs.

Warm Springs was a quiet place: wind through pine trees, no footsteps. The campus was leveled flat and gridded with sidewalks connecting low whitewashed buildings to each other. Mom pointed the way, and I pushed her toward the Outpatient Building. Wheelchair-bound people passed us by on the sidewalk, energetically transporting themselves, crisscrossing the campus, efficient and preoccupied.

"Here we are," Mom said, looking over her shoulder at me. She repositioned her braced leg on her foot pedal, testing for a more comfortable position. There wasn't anyone else here whose chair was pushed by a family member.

I tapped Mom's front pedals onto a guarding of thick clear plastic that was secured to the bottom of the Outpatient door. The door was oversized and made of light wood that sprang open effortlessly, like a weightless curtain. Mom's chair glided over the buffed linoleum floor of the building's wide hallway.

"Wow," I said, smiling and feeling as if the chair could propel itself.

"Just wait," Mom said, and I didn't know what she meant.

A woman sat behind a check-in desk at the end of the hall.

"Mrs. Saginaw! Welcome back," she shouted her greeting. "Oh, don't tell me." She grinned as we approached her desk. "This must be your daughter. I see the strong resemblance." The woman was slender and primly dressed in a blouse with a Peter Pan collar. Her blond hair was bobbed in a practical cut, and her shoulders were broad and squared, like Mom's, from years of maneuvering her wheelchair. Her bright lipstick and nails were shiny, and her friendly demeanor slightly overdone.

Normally I would bristle when people back in Dallas said I looked like Mom. It cut against my teenaged grain of independence-seeking. Anyway, I always thought the trait we shared most visibly was the dark circles under our eyes—shadows I would rather forget about. But in Warm Springs I felt differently about our appearance together. Here, I felt that I shared a sense of pride with the woman behind the desk. Mom was a Warm Springs success story, and I was a badge of her success. Mom bore me and raised me and didn't allow herself to be defined by polio. I sent a half smile to the woman behind her desk.

She shuffled through papers at the side of her typewriter and pulled out Mom's schedule. Together they reviewed the appointments: Dr. Bennett this afternoon, the brace shop and the corset shop the following morning, then a meeting with the physiotherapist before lunch in Georgia Hall.

"You'll be out of here in no time," she said, sliding the paper over her desktop.

Mom ran her eyes over the paper. "That's good news," she said without commentary. Mom had no specific requirements to explain or special arrangements to request. Mom's needs were identical to those of all the others who checked in at this welcoming station.

The two women looked at each other and their moods shifted. What they shared was hidden and veiled, like a secret handshake or the private communication of twins. I didn't understand the change in demeanor, but I knew that it had to do with a shared past. The woman reached across her desk for Mom's hand and cupped it in her own.

"It's okay now," she said in a soft voice, full of ambiguity.

My heartbeat slowed. I was an able-bodied exception at Warm Springs and separated from the complexities these women understood. They had outlasted the physical pain and social isolation of polio rehabilitation. They had endured paralysis and somehow outwitted death. Their atrophied legs and muscular shoulders, their wheelchairs and braces were reminders of their survival. I stared into the reflective buffed floor: the bond they shared was as inaccessible to me as my effortless gait was to them.

"Let's go, Mom," I said and returned my hands to her handlebars.

Dr. Bennett wore a white lab coat and wire-rimmed glasses and his hair was side parted and slicked back from his face. When he entered his office from a door behind his desk, he reminded me of Dr. Kildare on TV—kind and mild mannered, yet adoring of the spotlight. Mom waited at the side of his desk, resting her elbow on a stack of files, her back toward me. When he entered the room, she straightened her posture and leaned forward. I uncrossed my legs in the visitor's chair that I had pulled up against the back wall.

The doctor greeted Mom with vigor and friendliness, placing a hand on her shoulder and squeezing: "I'm glad to see you, Rose. You are looking very well." His voice resounded in the large, airy office. I couldn't see Mom's face, but I could tell by the way she raised her chin that she wore a tight smile: "I'm feeling good. Thank you. I brought my daughter here with me this year. Janie. She's in high school now."

Dr. Bennett barely glanced in my direction before squatting onto a stool that he rolled beside Mom's wheelchair. He took her wrist between his fingers and checked her pulse; he slid a stethoscope from his breast pocket and listened to her heart while assessing her face.

"It's okay, Rose, you can relax," he said. He touched her shoulder again.

Dr. Bennett jotted notes onto paper on his clipboard and stood up to evaluate Mom's posture from a distance. He ran his eyes from one of her shoulders to the other, back and forth several times. He puckered his mouth and circled her chair, his eyes never leaving sight of her torso. When he returned to his desk, he checked Mom's medical chart and heaved before he spoke.

"We need to tackle the scoliosis, Rose," he said, tapping his index finger on her file. "It's continuing to progress."

Mom checked the position of her brakes and didn't say anything.

I didn't know she had scoliosis. If Mom had ever mentioned the condition, it was probably in passing, and I didn't register it as anything to be concerned about. I never thought of Mom as unhealthy. Her wheelchair and leg brace were inconveniences, yes, but that was all. Some people had mothers who spoke with foreign accents. Mine used a wheelchair, but she wasn't sick. Not now. Long, long ago she was sick. That was an important part of the story:

I was a newlywed, three months pregnant with Harry when my neck stiffened and my legs buckled. My fever burned and I couldn't move. After Harry was born, I was so weak that I couldn't hold him in my arms. Then your father tricked me. He said he was taking me to Florida to get some rest. By now Harry was nine months old. Instead he drove me to Warm Springs and left me there. I cried and carried on. I didn't want to stay and leave my baby. But I got world-class treatment at Warm Springs. I had the same doctors as President Roosevelt. And I got better. They fitted me in proper braces and corsets, and I learned to live with confidence. I don't think of myself as sick. I'm not sick. By the time you were born, I was strong and healthy.

I never questioned the story or sought to fill in its gaps, but I absorbed the sadness embedded in everything that was never said. Mom had been deathly ill, and she eventually got better, thanks to Warm Springs. It was a devastating story that ended on a happy note. I had no interest in more details. It was too painful to imagine the suffering.

I looked across the office to Dr. Bennett standing behind his desk. If only he would acknowledge me by sending me a clue indicating Mom's condition—a reassuring wink or an expression of grave concern. He could have at least noticed that Mom and I resembled each other. But his eyes didn't meet mine. He held Mom's gaze and watched her as she released a slow breath.

"I'm going to fit you in a new style of corset this year," he said. "It's heavier and sturdier, with better supplemental support that will help slow the curvature."

I winced when Mom lifted her arm to interrupt her doctor.

"Dr. Bennett," Mom said, raising her red polished nail like a stop sign. "I believe my corset is fine. I think the problem is that my stays need replacing." Mom fisted her hand into her waist and pushed in on a metal stay that had bowed and, she believed, was allowing her spine to bend out of shape. "I need new stays. I honestly think that will fix the situation."

My face flushed and the blood rushing to my head blurred my thoughts. The audacity! This was Dr. Bennett! *The* Dr. Bennett. Wasn't he one of FDR's physicians? Wasn't he a world-renowned expert that made this place so exceptional? Now she was directing him on her scoliosis treatment?

But Dr. Bennett seemed unperturbed by Mom's assertiveness. He grinned as he stepped in next to her and placed a hand on her waist. He pressed into the metal bar on the side of her corset and stared into the floor behind her wheel.

"Doctor," Mom said. "I don't think I can handle a heavier corset."

"I see," Dr. Bennett said, still looking into the floor. "I see."

And I could see the candid communication between them. Dr. Bennett understood Mom's fear of change. Her corset was the first thing she put on in the morning and the last thing she removed at night. Without it strapped into place, she couldn't sit up straight—her back would curl over her distended stomach and she would fall to one side, losing balance. She had worn the same style of corset for more than twenty years. What if the new one didn't work? What if she couldn't adjust to its shape, its weight, its new requirements for dressing? What if Mom gave up her familiar corset and found herself newly dependent on other people to get dressed in the morning? What would it mean for the family? For her dignity? The doctor appreciated that Mom's corset held up more than her spine.

He slid his glasses up the bridge of his nose and stepped away from Mom's wheelchair. "You're dressing independently and transferring from your chair alone," he said. "This is essential, as you well know, for maintaining superior upper-body strength. We don't want to lose that capability in any way. You've got a good point there."

He returned to his desk and wrote a prescription for the old-style corset with new, thicker, reinforced stays. He encouraged her to lose ten pounds, watch her blood pressure, and nap every afternoon.

"You're doing very well, Rose," he said. "I want you to watch the ankle swelling. But I'm pleased with the way you're maintaining independence. We'll continue to monitor the scoliosis."

Only then did he look in my direction, hold my gaze, and nod. Only then did I hang my head. The two of us shared an understanding about Mom's psychological needs. We knew that satisfying them was more important to her health than attending to her physical ones. But the doctor had access to Mom's medical records; his perspective was supported by facts. He understood the progression of her paralysis and the obstacles she overcame to gain the mobility she had achieved. I was uninformed and only had soft stories to rely upon. In Dr. Bennett's nod to me, I sensed the volumes of medicals records that I would never open.

The next afternoon, I pushed Mom past the bubbly fountain and the grand columns of Georgia Hall and onto the building's creaking floor. She felt lighter in her realigned wheelchair and her spirits had lifted too now that we were almost headed home. Banquet tables extended down the middle of the hall under a high ceiling. Glasses brimmed with iced tea and the silverware shone. The smell of Southern cooking was comforting. The loosely folded napkins and the extra space around the china settings created a relaxed elegance. Maybe it was the fact that there weren't chairs pulled up to the waxed wooden tables that allowed for the airy, open feel.

"Far-out," I said, relieved to be away from the medical scene. "And I'm hungry."

It had been a wearying day. Mom had been measured and fitted for new corsets. Her leg brace was tightened at the knee hinge and adjusted at its base to fit her new saddle-oxford-style orthopedic shoes. The wheels on her chair were straightened and a new green woven seat replaced the old blue cracked vinyl one. I didn't go with Mom to her appointments. After the visit with Dr. Bennett, I realized she didn't need me for assistance here, and I didn't want to observe any more Warm Springs routine. I had seen enough. Once her name was called for consultations, I delivered her to an examination room and stepped outside. I sat on a bench, watching other polios hustle across campus: heads thrust forward, elbows jutting into the air, wheels spinning.

It was my impulse to hop up and help when Mom approached any physical challenge back home—a narrow passage, a steep slope, a closed door. I seemed to leap reflexively into service. But I didn't jump to the aid of anyone here. My eager availability felt too much like pandering. Nobody needed my assistance. No one even made eye contact with me. I looked into my lap when people wheeled near me, studied the weave of my blue jeans. Self-reliance was important currency at Warm Springs. I didn't just feel worthless, I was embarrassed by my patronizing attitude: I can walk. You can't. You must need me. It just wasn't the case at all! I was an invited guest here, not a physical crutch.

"Janie!" Mom called out when she finished with the physiotherapist. She labored toward me where I sat alone on a veranda. "I'm done, honey," she smiled. "All finished. Let's go!"

Mom's face was drawn and pale, and her attempt at sounding energetic was forced. I could only imagine what she heard in those examination rooms—she had lost too much strength, her muscle tone was slack, she was overweight, her equipment outdated, her circulation dangerously impaired. I couldn't evaluate her medically, but it was clear to me that her mental outlook differed from the others I had watched on campus. Her elbows didn't jut with the same enthusiasm; her wheels didn't spin at the accelerated pace. And Mom didn't avoid eye contact with me. No. Mom's eyes sought mine out like searchlights—seeking my support, her validation.

Mom rolled her chair beside my bench and we sat for a moment in the breeze, looking into the pines. Soon she snapped open her purse for her lipstick, stretched her mouth over her teeth, and drew a red crescent on her lower lip. Her chest rose when she checked herself in a makeup mirror. Back to Dallas! Finished and done with Warm Springs!

"Want to get lunch?" I asked. I didn't have the will to inquire about her appointments. I was as happy as she was to be finishing up here. And I was even happier with our silence.

"The food is good," Mom said.

When I steered her toward a communal table in Georgia Hall, Mom pointed me in a different direction, to a private table for two on the side of the room near a window.

"This is where Roosevelt hosted his Thanksgiving feasts, you know," she said.

Of course I knew about the famous hall. I recognized its elegance when I first stepped inside. Was it the *Life* magazine cover story that I had seen? Or was it that Mom had described the place to me so often that I had envisioned every detail? FDR propped up against the door with a cane, greeting polio patients with an outstretched arm and an off-center smile. This is where he carved his turkeys. This is where he delivered his address, assuring patients that disability did not diminish anyone's worth, nor should it hinder anyone's ambitions. Yes, of course I knew where we were. Georgia Hall was the center stage of the Warm Springs story.

"I was never here for Thanksgiving, but FDR sat over there—"

"Mom, I know," I interrupted her. "I know all about FDR."

I pushed her wheelchair up to the table she had selected. A server brought over a wicker-backed chair for me and told us about her lunch selections.

"Too bad the kitchen's not serving Daisy's Country Captain," Mom smiled up at her.

Daisy Bonner was FDR's cook at the Little White House in Warm Springs and Country Captain was the president's favorite meal. Mom liked to prepare Daisy's Country Captain when we had company for dinner in Dallas. "Roosevelt loved this meal!" Mom would repeat *every* time she served the dish. She'd curry chicken pieces and stir them into a tomato-and-pepper stew that she ladled over white rice and garnished with black currants and blanched almonds. It was an exotic recipe in the 1960s, when usual cuisine was tuna casseroles and Jell-O molds.

"You know Daisy's passed on, ma'am," our server said. "I knew her well. She let me stand to her side and cook some days." The woman shook her head and smiled the way people do when they are at a loss for words to describe an image. "She was a good woman. Something else."

Memories possessed people here. Maybe they weren't simply memories, maybe spirits were inside those past experiences that clung to the walls, crept from the floorboards, and swarmed the air of this hall. It was as if Warm Springs was haunted with polio patients. FDR cheering them on. A Southern cook stirring Creole stew. Doctors with nothing but leg braces to prescribe. The longer I sat in Georgia Hall, the more stifling the atmosphere became. By the time lunch arrived, my appetite had gone. I picked at the crust of my club sandwich.

"Janie, dear, I told you. The food's good." Mom reached for my hand. "Why aren't you eating?"

I couldn't tell Mom that I hated it here, when I knew she hated it more than I did. But I couldn't manage a pleasant disposition and pretend I was inspired by the pep talks of a long-dead president. I didn't want to tell Mom that I hurt for her. Sympathy would make her own pain worse. So I looked at Mom and presented her with a hollowed-out expression.

Mom tightened her red lips and stared back at me. Her eyes shone bright and the shadows under them were etched deep. She knew very well why I wasn't eating. She understood that I was overwhelmed. And I knew that she was overwhelmed also. But she was the one who brought me here. And now we were both trapped.

I practiced the question in my head before I spoke, rallying the courage to broach the subject of polio. My voice was stiff, but I managed to ask: "Did anyone ever figure out why some people got polio and others didn't?"

Mom squeezed my hand before letting it go.

"Bad luck," she answered and looked away.

"No, really," I persisted. "Why?"

"Polio is a virus. Who knows why anyone gets a virus?"

I stared at the magnolia printed on the rim of my plate and followed the pattern of white flowers around the circle. I'd be back home soon enough. I'd shut the door to my bedroom and plug in headphones and gaze out the window at wildflowers.

"Because W is a crooked letter," Mom said.

I wished I could just walk away. *Because W is a crooked letter* was the retort her father quipped to end her vexing questions as a child. Mom had said the same thing to me sometimes when I was younger. Back then the non sequitur sounded amusing, something from the Old World, but now it just sounded evasive.

"But why did some people recover and others stay paralyzed?" I asked, and the words were looser in my throat now.

Mom lifted her coffee cup from its saucer and her hand shook and the hot liquid rippled on the surface. She set the cup back in its place and raised her shoulders toward her ears.

"Because the world is round," she said, and her eyes reflected like mirrors.

Mom didn't flinch. She relaxed her face and looked as authentic as I had ever seen. Maybe it was a relief for her. We were finally talking about polio. I didn't sense that she was avoiding me. She was trying her hardest, doing her best to explain what she couldn't. Or wouldn't. I could almost hear the discordant thoughts bouncing around in her psyche: *I should have called the doctor earlier. My mother was superstitious. I was scared they'd abort my baby. I felt cursed. Fate ... God ... Dybbuks ... Punishment.*

Only then did I understand why she had brought me here. In her unguarded face I could see that Mom wanted me to understand her story, but not at the risk of her own unraveling. She had showed me the cover of this book called Warm Springs but was not prepared to open the pages.

My heart surged and hung low in my chest like a bag of sand. I accepted Mom's nonanswer. The world *is* round. It *does* spin. Seasons shift and so do people's understanding of things. Mom's polio experience was hers, not mine. This place, Warm Springs, was her story to tell. It wasn't me who was abandoned here, bedbound.

Sunlight streamed in through the window and one side of Mom's face glowed. *I got better at Warm Springs. FDR inspired us.*

The world is round. What a true and beautiful story; what a magnificent rendering of reality. This tale occupied Mom's psychic space and forced darker stories to the background. And now I realized that the same tale could protect me and free me from the duty of absorbing more pain. I pushed the crumbs from my sandwich away from my plate and into a pile in the middle of our table. I felt closer to her and as far away as ever.

I took a bite of my sandwich. "I can sort of picture Roosevelt over there," I said. "It's like he's sitting at that long table now, slicing turkey."

Unanswered questions churned inside me as Mom and Dad and I returned to the Metropol after our meeting with Dr. Kadelburg. I was happy to find Harry in the hotel's lobby among the pacing chess players. Harry had relaxed into a chair and was reading the *International Herald Tribune* that he bought in the Athens airport. He would be able to clarify things, shine some light on my confusion about Dr. Kadelburg and the Iron Curtain: Was there an actual physical barrier or was The Iron Curtain a way of talking? Did there exist a partition that divided free people from those not free or was it an unseen boundary that was more obvious in some places than others? Were the people of Yugoslavia *partially* free? And I was eager to show Harry the books Dr. Kadelburg gave us after Dad made a contribution to the Federation of Jewish Communities. Maybe we could leaf through the Sarajevo Haggadah together while Harry explained the history of the Spanish Inquisition and theorized on the book's circuitous route to Yugoslavia. Then I'd tell Harry how Mom froze up and refused to open Dr. Kadelburg's black book of World War II atrocities. I imagined Harry would scoff, "Yeah, Mom's view of history is selective." I imagined he would smirk and that I would smirk too.

"Bobby Fischer won three to one against Petrosian," Harry said when he saw me, before I had a chance to say anything. "Unbelievable! An American beat the Soviet! Just incredible, Jane! Journalists here are already calling this game the Match of the Century."

"Yeah?" I said and slouched onto the couch next to him. I was annoyed with chess and impatient with Harry's obsession with the game, but I placed talking about Dr. Kadelburg on hold. My jumbled thoughts couldn't compete against Harry's enthusiasm. "I don't understand why a board game is such a big deal," I finally said. "It just seems really stupid to me."

"Not at all," Harry said, shaking his head at my ignorance. "Think of it this way. Here are some of the smartest people in the world." Harry gestured with his paper at the men in the lobby, still pacing the marble floor. "They sit across from each other at a table. They don't speak the same language. And they play this intense game, moving pieces on a black and white board, trying to outstrategize each other. They represent different countries. The stakes are as high as it gets."

"So what?" Harry wasn't making any sense to me, and I had enough on my mind already.

"That's huge, Jane. Think. Someone wins. He outwits the other. Someone loses. The outcome is clear-cut. There is no ambiguity."

I had zero interest in what Harry was saying. Black and white boxes. Winners and losers. These smart men in suits seemed ridiculous, circling the floor, agonizing over their moves on a board. Clear-cut outcomes? Nothing seemed clear-cut to me. The visit with Dr. Kadelburg had raised questions that I knew could only be answered with fuzzy responses, if there were any answers at all.

"I'll tell you what makes the game intriguing," Harry said, leaning forward and jiggling his knee. "Everybody sees the exact same thing. Every chess move is observed and recorded. Once a play is made it can't be changed. No one can come back and spin a tale about what they think really happened."

"Yeah," I said and yawned. I glanced at the newspaper. Skirmishes along the border with Cambodia were raising international concerns that the war might spread beyond the confines of Vietnam. New international boundaries had been crossed and the Vietnam War was expanding. "I guess it all depends on how you look at it."

THIRTEEN

London, England
May 9–10, 1970

"BUT YOU DON'T GET IT, DAD."

"I get it, plenty. Believe me, I do. It's obscene."

"It's the Beatles! This is London!"

Mom and Dad and I were drinking Cokes in the lobby of the Westbury Hotel on New Bond Street and I wanted to go to the John Lennon exhibit that was just down the street. We had arrived in London a few days previous, this being the last stop on our trip before returning to Dallas. Harry had already gone back to Austin to take his law school exams. The exhibition of Lennon's lithographs was a big international sensation—shocking because of its explicitness. But without Harry as an ally, it felt futile arguing for permission to go see it. Dad never appreciated the Beatles, anyway. To him, they were just a long-haired British quartet that turned everything about music upside down. It's not that he disliked them, he just didn't understand why they were so important. He had no idea that I always had a Beatles song playing somewhere in my head: *All you need is love. I believe in yesterday. Help! I need somebody!*

I was ten years old in 1964 when the Beatles first appeared on *The Ed Sullivan Show* in their dark suits and Beatle boots, singing "I

Want to Hold Your Hand." They bounced around the stage, heads cocked, grinning and harmonizing. I had bought every Beatles album as soon as it was released and listened to them incessantly.

Harry and I had read about Lennon's solo show, *Bag One, The Erotic Lithographs,* in the international newspapers months earlier. The day after the exhibit opened, back in January, Scotland Yard shut it down and confiscated eight of the fourteen lithographs. A judge had determined that the drawings were pornographic and ruled that the show was indecent for public display. But now a higher court had just reversed that finding and held that entrance into the gallery was a voluntary act and that Lennon's art was neither public nor obscene. The lithographs were returned to the gallery, but there was still confusion about what was on display. The press coverage continued, and my curiosity mounted with each headline.

"It's not like I've never seen a drawing of a naked woman before," I said to Dad. "I mean, look at Picasso. He does it all the time."

"Picasso's not pornography," Dad said. "Picasso isn't obscene." He rubbed the back of his neck and motioned to our waitress to bring him the bar tab.

She smiled from across the room and walked toward our table with a lighthearted, breezy gait. She was a cool mod à la Carnaby Street, wearing white stretchy hot pants with back fishnets. Her white leather boots were squared off at the toes and zipped up the inside of her leg to the middle of her calves. Her blond hair hung to the top of her shoulders and bangs fell Mary Quant style into her thick lashes. She spoke to Dad in a low whispery voice and Dad smiled at her in amusement as he paid our bill.

"So, is she obscene?" I asked Dad as soon as our waitress turned away. "I can see her legs. Woo-woo."

"Jane," Mom said. "Just drop it." Mom had been quiet about the Lennon show ever since I brought up the subject, and I wasn't sure how she felt about seeing it. She was fascinated by the Beatles; she always wanted me to explain the lyrics. In fact, I thought she was too curious. The Beatles were mine, Mom.

Oh well, we were going home soon. Even sooner than we had originally planned. When we'd arrived in London, there was a telegram waiting for Dad at the front desk. Some business issue had arisen with the Brake-O deal, and the new owners needed Dad's input. It was not anything that would sink the deal, but it was important enough that Mom had called Pan Am and was trying to rebook us on an earlier flight back to Dallas. *Dallas.* It was hard to imagine.

"Dad, I'm sixteen."

"And I'm grossed out with all the hippie rigmarole around here," he said.

"I'm going for a walk," I said and pushed away from the table. My pink cotton tunic that I had bought in India dropped over my knees when I stood up. I realized that the frayed hem of my blue jeans had taken on the look of an authentic traveler's garment. I wasn't just an American kid making a fashion statement.

Dad gave me some money and told me to be back in an hour. "Just be careful out there," he said and immediately turned his head and started talking to Mom about Brake-O.

I walked over to the London Arts Gallery at 22 New Bond and lingered on the sidewalk. A single framed black-and-white lithograph hung in the window, a squiggly cartoonlike self-portrait of John Lennon. That was it. A group of gawkers clustered around it, snickering and poking their elbows into each other's side. They were mostly men in business dress, white shirts with skinny black ties and slicked-back short hair. I wondered why they didn't just go inside if they were so amused by the whole thing. They were adults. They didn't need anyone's permission.

A man in a dark suit with a barrel-shaped chest held his hands stiffly in front of his waist, guarding the entrance. He clenched his jaw and narrowed his eyes and glared his disapproval at me. His stern judgment reminded me of Dad's. My face burned pink as I looked away from the guard. As much as I wanted to, I couldn't ignore that man's towering presence. I didn't have the courage to pass beyond him and enter the gallery alone. Instead, I adjusted my Peter Max scarf, flattened my bangs to my forehead, and wandered over to Oxford Street, heading for Hyde Park.

Crocuses bloomed in neat rows under the daffodils in the flower-beds across from Marble Arch, but that was the extent of imposed order at the Speakers' Corner at Hyde Park. The sidewalks were packed and the atmosphere was free-flowing. Every few steps some-one plopped down a soapbox, climbed up on top of it, and spouted out an opinion or told a long tale. A man with a full white beard bal-anced on his tiptoes, waved a worn Bible, and foretold the end of the world. A waif of a woman stood next to him, pale and demure in tat-tered espadrilles, whispering the virtues of her fruitarian diet. There were Maoists and Buddhists, poets and love children with flowers in their hair. I'd never seen such a mix of humanity. I didn't get to Woodstock, but look where I found myself now! I felt wonderfully at home in my worn jeans, with my Indian caftan rippling in the breeze. John Lennon's "Give Peace a Chance" popped into my mind:

> Everybody's talking about
> Bagism, Shagism, Dragism, Madism, Ragism, Tagism

This-ism, That-ism, ism ism ism
All we are saying is give peace a chance!

At the Speakers' Corner, free expression was the only thing that mattered. The content of what was said seemed secondary to the act of speaking your mind. What a relief. I had been feeling stifled ever since we left Yugoslavia. Mom, Dad, Harry, and I had flown from Belgrade to Vienna and rented a car there. We went on to Germany, Denmark, Sweden, Holland, and France. A few days here. A few days there. We drove through dark forests in a four-door Audi. We spotted castles on hilltops in the countryside. We slept under fluffed-up down comforters in elegant hotels and tasted truffles and fancy cheeses.

At the Three Falcons, a candlelit restaurant in the center of Copenhagen, Dad selected grouse from the handwritten menu. "It should be like a pheasant," Mom surmised. Our nervous waiter smiled and hovered. He bowed from the waist as he placed a porcelain plate under a large silver dome in front of Dad. Ta! Da! We laughed hysterically at the forlorn little bird that elicited the pomp of our white-gloved waiter. There was something absurd about the out-of-proportion formality encircling the scrawny little creature. But when the laughing stopped, the image of the little bird lingered. What was it? In some way, I identified with the grouse's immobility and its isolation there in the center of a plate, the way it was trapped in opulence. I was uncomfortable in Europe. I longed to be back in India or Israel, Turkey or Yugoslavia—someplace where I felt a connection to the surroundings and life was less pretentious. For all the elegant show that was Europe, I became subdued as we made our way from country to country. I felt detached, mismatched, and lonely, like that tiny bird on a giant plate.

Europe stirred up a yearning for home. It began in Stockholm. We arrived there in the middle of April, as President Nixon was authorizing American troops to enter Cambodia, expanding the Vietnam War effort. Anti-war protests were sparked across university campuses in the United States and were spreading through European capitals. When we checked into our hotel, Harry got word that a rally was organized for that afternoon in Stockholm's main square just in front of our hotel. I begged to go with him, but he wouldn't let me. "You're not old enough for a demonstration, Jane. Anyway, I want to meet some locals," he smiled. When I didn't back down, Harry let up, but with strict instructions: "If anyone asks you where you're from, don't say you're American. Say you're from Canada. Better yet, just don't talk at all." Of course I agreed and followed Harry, tagging a few steps behind him at the demonstration. Everyone was chanting "No more war!" and waving placards with peace signs. I tried to act like I belonged, wrinkling my forehead and suppressing any urge to smile.

Then there was my sixteenth birthday in Amsterdam. We went to a Passover seder at the home of a Dutch family who had relatives we knew in Dallas. It was a large, happy gathering of about twenty people. The Haggadah was printed in Dutch and Hebrew, and the cute boy seated next to me guided me through the book. He read the Hebrew with a thick Dutch accent, and then I read it with an exaggerated Texas drawl. We thought we were very funny. He had bright blue eyes and an off-center flirty grin. After the seder, he asked if he could take me out the next night for my birthday. I was thrilled.

We met in the lobby of our hotel and walked to a neighborhood restaurant. Our steps were out of sync and we mostly stumbled with our words. We smiled our way through the meal. He ordered us beers, and I acted like that was normal, even though I'd never had more than a couple of sips on my own. I couldn't tell if I liked him or not, but I loved going out on my birthday. After dinner, the Dutch boy reached for my hand, and we strolled beside a canal watching the lights from row houses reflect off the water. Our palms were moist. Bicycles wheeled slowly by us, and we squeezed our hands tighter together. I tilted my head toward his shoulder. Maybe we could say with our mouths what we couldn't speak with our language. He gestured and I happily turned my face to his. But the boy tasted bitter and his tongue jutted aggressively into my mouth. I pushed him away. "American!" he scoffed. He walked me back to our hotel, and we didn't even pretend to talk. I was lonelier than before we had met.

There was a painting on display at the Louisiana Museum in the woods an hour outside of Copenhagen that captured my internal landscape in Europe. The painting by Marc Chagall was entitled *Time Is a River without Banks*:

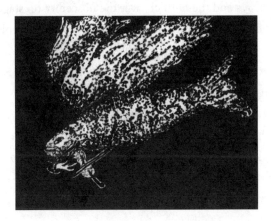

I stood inches from the painting and studied it: a fish out of water, flying solo. That muscular fish, flapping across the canvas, had left its home too. A remote village on the riverbanks was barely discernible on the horizon. And even though the fish's destination was unknown, it played a fiddle in midair, seemingly content as it traveled forward. Would that fish ever go back to its home? Unlikely, I thought. I wondered how Dallas would seem when I finally returned, having flown around the world.

"I've got tickets for tonight's *Hair*," said the man who approached me in Hyde Park. "Interested?" He was wearing purple corduroy bell-bottoms, a sweater vest, and a string of love beads around his neck. His hair fell to his shoulders, and he had on those leather sandals with a toe ring like the ones Harry and I had bought in New Delhi. He looked like he could jump on stage and be part of the production.

I was stunned for a moment. *Hair*? Me? I had the album at home and knew the words to all the songs, but I never thought I would ever see the play. Everybody knew about the nude scenes and the drugs and the hubbub over the obscenity on stage. Did I want tickets to *Hair*? Who wouldn't? But my parents would never let me.

"How much are they?" I asked. The lyrics of "Let the Sunshine In" began playing in my head.

"Orchestra tickets. Twenty pounds."

Dad had given me ten pounds when I left the hotel and that seemed like a lot of money. Was this guy trying to cheat me? Maybe he wasn't a real love child. Maybe he was a huckster, preying on tourists, and I looked like a tourist to him, not a hippie at all.

"No thanks," I said.

"But it's the Age of Aquarius, lovey."

"I'm not interested."

"It's now or never, you know."

When he smiled, I hardened my gaze. I returned to my habit of self-protection. Why was I closing myself off so suddenly? Harry would have grabbed up a ticket. He would have bargained with this guy and cut some sort of deal. And Mom and Dad weren't around here, hovering and telling me what to do. I was free! This was Hyde Park! I was about to return to high school and this guy was offering me an experience that would never come my way again.

"I don't have twenty pounds. Do you have anything cheaper?"

"The balcony's five pounds."

I don't know whether the sunshine in the park brightened. And I'm not certain if the birds really began to chirp more loudly from the trees. But I sensed a veil had lifted from around me and I stood in the middle of the park, exposed and fully alive.

"Okay. I'll take one seat." I dug into my shoulder bag for the money.

He handed me a ticket from the pocket of his corduroys and I turned it over several times, inspecting it carefully—*Hair: The American Tribal Love-Rock Musical, Shaftesbury Theatre, Eight o'clock.*

"Get there early," he said. "It's real, love."

Dad was nonplussed when I told him I had a ticket for that evening's performance of *Hair,* but he didn't say I couldn't go. "Spoiled brats. They ought to be ashamed of themselves running around naked," he said.

Mom was more circumspect. "It might be very interesting," she said and raised an eyebrow. "The play captures this moment in history, that's for sure." She gazed over my shoulder, as if checking herself in a mirror. She didn't say anything else, but I got the clear impression by the slow smile she kept contained, that she was rather proud of my show of independence.

I climbed to the top balcony of the Shaftesbury and dropped into a velvet seat just as the house lights switched off and the theater went silent. A deep gong vibrated through the darkness. Then delicate chimes joined in. When the lights flipped on, a happening began! Oh, there was a plot—about a boy named Claude who got drafted for the war in Vietnam—but the plot only served as loose background structure for the music and merriment of Claude's tribe of rebellious anti-war friends. *Hair* was all about music and youthful liberation from adult expectations. *This is the dawning of the Age of Aquarius,* the tribe of friends sang with abandon. *Harmony and understanding, sympathy and trust abounding.* It was an anti-war extravaganza—beads and feathers and flags—and at the end of the second act, the audience was called onto the stage as part of a live Be-In. I couldn't believe it! I found myself center stage, waving my arms over my head, swaying with the cast and the rest of the audience. I belted out "Let the Sunshine In" as if I was in the leading role. Was this really me? My smile was ecstatic.

My hips swung loose as I walked from the theater back to the Westbury. My stride was sure-footed as I leapt toward my endpoint. I remembered a night in Paris a few weeks earlier. We had arrived at our hotel to find that our reservation had been canceled, and the manager corrected the mistake by booking us into the presidential suite. The carpet was too thick for Mom's wheelchair to roll across. The marble tub was too cold against my back for me to take a bath. I climbed a footstool to my bed, but the feather duvet felt weightless, too light to sleep under. I passed the night peering through the wrought iron of our balcony into a streetlamp. At dawn, a man in a beret pedaled down the street on his bicycle. He thumbed a bell attached to his handlebars. There were baguettes shoved under his armpits. I watched him cycle to the end of our block, park his bike, and hop off his seat to begin his day's work delivering bread. In my sleepless stupor, I thought that this was the most beautiful scene I could imagine. The man was at ease, clear about his place in an orderly world. In London after the show, I felt like that man: at ease with myself.

When I turned onto New Bond, I stopped again and lingered in front of the Lennon exhibit. The gallery was closed and the sidewalk in front was empty. The display had been changed, and now a single light shone on a lithograph depicting John and Yoko together in a loose embrace. Yoko was smiling and her eyes were closed like a tranquil child's. The simplicity of the drawing was lovely. I was determined to return the next day.

"Janie," Mom called the next morning from her bedroom at the Westbury. "Can you help me with my bra?"

I ignored the summons. The morning was quiet, and Dad had gone down to the gym. I sat cross-legged in a Queen Anne chair in the living room of our suite, watching a BBC special on our black-and-white TV. It was official: the Beatles had broken up. Paul McCartney had said as much in an interview the month before, but now the reality of the group's demise was starting to sink in. The London media was obsessed, as if there was no other story to cover. It was the end of an era, and I thought my world would never be the same again.

"Janie!"

I looked through the bedroom door and Mom was lying on her back, facing the ceiling, her legs dangling over the side of her bed toward the carpet.

"I need some help," she said.

I delayed before I stood up.

"Help! I need somebody!" I crooned, shaking my head like a Beatle as I walked toward her. I was aggressively playful—*Neeeeeed somebody*—condescendingly sarcastic.

"Give me a hand," Mom said, and she raised her arms toward the door as I passed through it. I stood beside her wheelchair, between her bare legs, and pulled her up into a sitting position. Her corset was already tied tightly into place and her breasts hung limply over the white canvas.

"I'm tired," Mom said. She leaned over and grabbed her bra from the seat of her wheelchair and handed it to me.

"The Beatles broke up," I said as I took the bra from her. "The end. It's real."

"Nothing's forever."

I climbed behind her on the bed as she lifted her breasts into the cups of her Maidenform longline. I pulled the elastic sides together and connected the hooks and eyes.

Mom stared forward as I dressed her.

"Your father and I have conferred," she said when I finished my job.

Conferred? I sighed. Now what?

"Tomorrow we leave for New York," Mom went on. "We'll spend this morning getting packed up. This afternoon we'll go by and visit that John Lennon art show."

I looked out over her shoulder into the open space of the living room. The BBC special was still playing, and the commentators were debating the cause of the Beatles' break up. Was Yoko Ono the culprit? And John Lennon by extension? Or was it Paul McCartney who had strayed from the group and destroyed the Beatles forever?

And now, what would become of this generation? What would unify the youth of today, the commentators queried, now that the revolutionary force of the Beatles had come to an end? I climbed out from behind Mom on the bed and went to turn off the TV.

"Honey," she said as I was walking away. "I have plenty of pish bags. Be sure to pack the extra toilet paper from your bathroom."

Dad stood outside the gallery and leaned against the brick wall with his arms crossed at his chest. I pushed Mom through the entrance onto the dark-stained floor. The eighteen Lennon lithographs hung at eye level, evenly dispersed in one room against stark white walls. We were the only visitors. Strange. This was John Lennon, and we were in London. Where were all the fans?

"Well," Mom said. "Let's see what all the to-do is about."

The floor creaked under Mom's wheels. *All the to-do.* I didn't want her to be here. I thought I'd visit the gallery by myself, as a sort of final farewell to this journey. Me, alone, at the center of my generation. The end of our trip. The end of the Beatles. I felt a sort of melancholy delight at the synchronicity. But Mom's presence crowded my spirit. Her excitement left no room for mine in the empty gallery.

The first frame was a line drawing of John Lennon's face. It had the simple lines of Japanese calligraphy. Too simple, I thought, to evoke a reaction. I pushed Mom passed several other frames: arches of India ink floating on white paper. What was the big deal? As we proceeded around the gallery, the images grew more complex. A sketch of John and Yoko signing their marriage license looked a lot like a cartoon from one of Mom's *New Yorker* magazines. We moved to the frames on another wall.

There it was: a drawing of Yoko Ono, naked and splayed wide

on her bed, her breasts toward the ceiling and her legs opened in an exaggerated V. Her hand reached to her crotch and her expression was one of pure ecstasy. Mom cleared her throat and I looked away from the drawing. This wasn't anything like a Picasso painting. Picasso's women were naked, but they weren't aroused. I was embarrassed and stunned. I pushed Mom forward without saying anything. More masturbation. More hairy details. Cunnilingus. A ménage à trois. I was so glad that I couldn't see Mom's face, and even happier that Dad was outside on the sidewalk. My groin ballooned. I wanted out of the gallery. I had never seen a penis before, and now I was looking at one with my mother.

I wished my parents had forbidden me access. Then I could have gotten angry. I could be outraged at the way they didn't understand me and my generation. I could have pouted and protested and not had to endure this embarrassment. I imagined Dad tapping his foot on the sidewalk.

"Let's go, Mom."

I was relieved to leave the exhibit. I was ready, in fact, to return to Dallas. The image of being in my room behind a shut door, stretched out on my bed with earphones, made my blood flow more evenly. I would sing along to *Abbey Road* in the privacy of my own space—*I know you. You know me. One thing I can tell you is you got to be free!* Home. I pulled in a deep breath and held it. I didn't know where I belonged anymore.

FOURTEEN

Dallas, Texas
1970 – 2022

1. Summer 1970

I SAT DOWN ON THE FRONT row of Texas civics in a pair of fringed denim shorts and crossed my legs. I had on yellow flip-flops and a gray T-shirt from the previous summer's Texas International Pop Festival. The air was static without a cooling system and dark rings spread from under my arms. Our teacher, Coach Daniels, stood so close to the edge of my desk that I could smell the snuff that sprayed from his mouth when he spoke.

"The Texas Legislature is a bicameral body," he said. "It meets on a biennial basis."

He turned and walked to his desk, plopped into the squeaky chair, and kicked his cowboy boots up onto the desktop. The tips pointed to a Confederate flag pinned behind him on the corkboard. Another rebel flag was stitched onto his shirt over the breast pocket. We were the Thomas Jefferson Rebels.

"That means there is a Senate and a House of Representatives and that they meet every *other* year," he continued and peered over his boots, scanning the six of us in his class.

The boy in the desk next to mine was a star on the T.J. football team. He must have flunked civics the first time, which put him in summer school. His blond hair was buzzed around his ears and tiny beads of sweat collected like freckles on his nose. He raised his hand and spoke without being called on. "Why, Coach?" he asked. "Why not meet every year?" Then looked at me and smirked. Wasn't he clever?

Coach swung his feet to the floor and leaned on his desk, digging his elbows into the wood top. "It doesn't matter why," he said. He wagged his head from side to side when he said *why* and exaggerated the pronunciation as if he was saying a foreign word—like *pourquoi*. "*Why* is not on the test," he went on. "I'm telling you what's on the test. And it is not *why*."

I looked at my classmate from the corner of my eye and smiled back.

"Is that funny, missy?" the coach asked me. "Is that funny to you?"

The boy wiped the sweat from his nose and I lowered my gaze and focused on the blond grain of my desktop. I didn't want to agitate Coach. I just wanted to get the school credit I needed to move forward with my graduating class of 1972. That was the arrangement Mom and Dad had negotiated with Mr. Smith before we left Dallas last January. I could withdraw after the first semester of sophomore year and reregister the next fall as an incoming junior, as long as I completed Texas civics over the summer.

"Read pages two hundred to two twelve," Coach said. "Memorize it. All of it." The coach wiggled a tin of snuff from his back pocket and pinched some more under his lower lip. He glanced out the window beyond the treeless courtyard. "I'll be right back," he said. "And no talking. I'll flunk you boys. You'll never see that football field again!"

He huffed through the door and I flung open my textbook. I liked the way the pages clumped together and the thick chemical smell they emitted. It seemed amazing that there was so much to write about Texas government. I flipped through the clumps until I came to page two hundred. Then I lowered my head and closed my eyes and fell into the murky aroma of high school.

I showed up for the first day of my junior year in a green plaid miniskirt and white ribbed turtleneck, clothes identical to those of most of the other girls in my class. I balanced my notebook against my right hip when I walked down the hall with the same nonchalance as the cheerleaders and drill team majorettes. We had all caked silver-blue shadow on our eyelids, and we crossed our right leg over our left when sat at our desks.

By lunchtime, I had already had my fill of being back in high school. I noticed Maryanne leave the building to sit outside in the grass while the rest of our class headed past the courtyard to the lunchroom. I recognized Maryanne from sophomore year. She lived on Woodfin, around the corner from me on Woodford, but we didn't know each other very well. She was a high-honor student, and our classes weren't scheduled together. She was wearing a long floral granny gown that fluttered over her huaraches when she walked. She didn't have stiff Dippity-do hair like me and the other girls. Her light brown hair hung parted down the middle with a natural wave and some frizz. I remembered her as soft-spoken and giggly, with a luster to her eyes that made her appear like she was halfway somewhere else, on the brink of a discovery. It was like Maryanne heard sounds that nobody else had access to. I liked her. I walked over to her in the grass just as she unpacked a sandwich from her brown paper bag.

"Can I sit with you?" I asked. "I forgot lunch money."

I tugged on my miniskirt and sat down on the ground beside her. I wasn't sure she remembered me.

"The sun feels good," I said.

Maryanne offered me a Frito. "I don't want to go to the lunch-room," she said. "The smell of overcooked vegetables. I can't take it anymore."

We watched the boys practice football across the street. Coach Daniels stood in the middle of the empty field with a baseball hat pulled low onto his forehead. He yelled, "HUP! HUP!" and the boys ran around him in circles.

"I went to Aspen this summer," Maryanne said. "To a music festival."

She described the scene so beautifully: fields of wildflowers, snow-capped mountains, long purple sunsets, and barefoot hippies in the park.

"It was like living inside a book of poetry," Maryanne said.

"Far out," I said. It was hard to know what to say or how to imagine her experience in Aspen. But her dimple deepened, and her eyes widened as she spoke, and I could tell that the summer had had a huge impact on her.

Maryanne and I smiled at each other. We picked at the grass in the courtyard. I crumbled a clod of dirt into dust and watched a group of ants, steadfast in formation, building a mound as a fortress.

"I went to Afghanistan last year," I said. "With my Mom and Dad and my brother. Women there wear these long colorful burkas that cover their whole body. They walk down the street, and you can't know who they really are." I wanted to share with her how awkward it was being back in school, but I didn't know where to begin. The bell rang and lunch break was over. "You know they are

there," I said, "but you can't see them." We stood up and went back
inside to our separate classes.

That night, I had a dream.

*I am at a party. It is in a mansion with a circular staircase, a cascad-
ing chandelier, and a string quartet. The men are wearing tuxedoes and
the women are in long gowns with their hair twisted into buns. I don't
know anyone and feel out of place.*

*The night air is balmy. I walk past the music to a veranda overlook-
ing a forest and lean onto the balustrade. A boy approaches and leans
next to me, touching my arm.*

He is blind.

*We talk awhile and he asks if he can show me something in the
forest. We cradle our elbows into each other's and descend the stairs,
stepping onto a dirt path. The boy knows exactly where he is going. He
points the way and I guide him there with my elbow. We step off the
path and walk over to a tree. A large gold-leafed frame hangs from its
trunk on a hook.*

"Do you see it?" the boy asks.

*I tell him I see a beautiful gold frame and a canvas that is painted
white.*

"It is my portrait," he says. "I thought maybe you could see it."

*We turn around, disappointed, and walk back to the party together,
elbow in elbow.*

When I woke up, I couldn't shake the dream's images. It was
puzzling because I had never been to a formal ball, and I didn't
know anyone who was blind. I knew the dream was filled with
meaning that I needed to sort through. I was a helper in the dream,
struggling to share what only the blind boy could see. That was

something I definitely understood. Perhaps the dream was clarifying the limits of my role as a caretaker and underscoring that I could never fully appreciate another's experience. Everyone's experiences are theirs alone. But then, maybe I was the blind boy. Maybe it was me, alone, who could see myself! Or maybe the boy and I were one and the same, trying to understand what it means to be visible. I lingered in bed, turning and turning the dream.

When I got to school, I found Maryanne by the flagpole in the courtyard before first period. I rushed over to her and described the gold-framed canvas on the tree in the forest. I told her about the blind boy in a tuxedo and my feeling of disappointment and how the dream wouldn't go away.

"Huh," she said. "Sounds like Aldous Huxley. *The Doors of Perception.*" But she was in a rush for a meeting, and we didn't have time to talk. I looked over at the other students loitering at the flagpole and resolved not to tell anyone else about my dream.

I remained in a stupor for most of that day. I sat alone in the lunchroom, perplexed that I couldn't see what that blind boy had tried to show me. I felt so close to grasping what he saw. Maybe if we had stayed longer in the forest the image would have emerged. Maybe I should have asked him to describe the colors and the shapes. I finally decided that I understood the dream: it was all about my frustrations. I wanted to see more but couldn't. I yearned to look beyond what my eyes allowed. *I* was the disabled one, not the blind boy. He saw himself perfectly. Maryanne was probably right about Aldous Huxley. I feared that the doors of my perception had been shut and that I was stuck back in Dallas.

At the end of the school day, I flung my books into my locker and kicked the metal door closed. I rotated the dial on my lock.

Maybe my body had landed back in high school, but my mind could still wander to far-flung places. I imagined the vastness of all I could not see and wondered about all the ways there were to look at the world. I refused to be trapped by my high school. Trapped in my miniskirt and silver-blue eye shadow.

When I returned home from school that afternoon I went to my room and closed the door. I sang along to *Abbey Road*: *I know you. You know me.* I had connected with that boy in my dream. I was offered a glimpse into a different way of seeing and I couldn't quite make the leap. But yet the two of us continued down a path together. Our gait unmistakably compatible. Maybe our synchronized walking was the key to this conundrum: we held on to each other. We grabbed each other's arms and we didn't let go.

2. June 2009

Forty years had passed since I was a junior and a dreamer at Thomas Jefferson High School. I stood at the foot of a rented hospital bed in Mom's apartment in Dallas and leaned into its metal railing. Mom hung in midair above the mattress, cradled in the blue mesh swing of a Hoyer lift. She was eighty-three years old and dying of metastatic cancer. Hospice had been called and attendants stayed with her around the clock. Mom's twig legs dangled. She no longer wore a leg brace, because she no longer had strength to stand. But Mom had not forgone her bright red lipstick. And her thick hair was styled into a neat gray wave. Her blue eyes were clear as she stared into me.

"The malekhamoves is in the other room," Mom said. She spoke in a raspy whisper and narrowed her eyes. She held me in her line of vision, and I stared right back at her. Mom shifted her focus to the bedroom door and pointed her finger and chin through the doorframe to the living room.

"It's flapping its wings in there right now," she said. "Circling. Waiting."

The Angel of Death. This wasn't the first time Mom had sighted it. But usually the malekhamoves arrived when Mom was alone, and I would hear about the visits in the past tense. *The malekhamoves was here last night and I beat him away from my window.* Or, *I saw the malekhamoves at my door. I slammed it shut and scared it away.* Mom seemed to enjoy recounting her dramatic tales of triumph in the dark. She would wrestle down the Angel of Death from her windowsill or bedpost and proudly report the conquest. My job was to listen, to nod, to cajole or distract her.

Just the day before she had reported that Dad had visited her.

"Your father was here last night," she said when I pulled up a chair for our afternoon chat. My father had died of lung cancer ten years earlier, in June of 1998.

"How *is* Dad?" I asked.

"Fine," Mom said. "He's fine." She slid her hand over the top of her bed sheet and straightened out the wrinkles. It was as if she was beckoning him to her side. "But this bed they gave me is too narrow. So he left." She sighed and changed the subject: "Now tell me, how are your kids?"

So when Mom hung in midair and pointed at the Angel of Death flapping its wings in her living room, I thought I knew exactly what to do. I assumed she was instructing me to intercede and to confront the malekhamoves on her behalf. To chase it away, *Shoo! Shoo!* Why else would she announce its presence in midday? What else would she be alerting me to? I lifted my weight from the railing of her bed.

"Let me close the door," I said.

"No," Mom said, shaking her head. "I like it there—"

The hospice nurse released a switch on the Hoyer lift and lowered Mom onto the mattress. She untied Mom's orthopedic shoes and fluffed up a pillow that she slipped between Mom atrophied legs. She tucked a cotton blanket over Mom's frail shoulders and brushed the hair back from her forehead. I watched. How strange it was to observe someone else taking such good care of my mother. Doing my job, I thought. And I felt a tremendous relief. It occurred to me that Warm Springs was the only other place I had felt free allowing another person attend to Mom's physical needs. I remembered being surprised that Mom was so relaxed in another's care when she felt assured that they understood polio and were not confused by the dynamics of her wheelchair. This hospice nurse was as comfortable with the needs of the dying as Warm Springs personnel were with the world of polio. In both instances, it seemed, there was a hint of performance involved as well. As if these caretakers wanted to demonstrate something: You see, Jane, you aren't the only qualified one.

I wheeled Mom's empty chair away from the side of her bed and pulled up a seat next to the railing. I hesitated before I reached for her wrinkled hand.

"The gates are locked," Mom said when I touched her. She squeezed my palm and let it go. She looked away from me through her bedroom window into the rose garden. Weary as I was, I couldn't leave Mom's side. I listened to her breathing as she fell asleep and wondered what gates she was referring to. Who was locked in and who was locked out?

I stayed seated at her bedside near her empty wheelchair and studied the way the spokes stretched from the metal rim to the gray rubber hub at its center. That wheel was as much a part of me as it was an extension of her. The neat symmetry of that crisscrossed circle was my first memory. And now, at age fifty-five, I still found comfort in the stable geometry of those wheels—a supporting structure that bound me and Mom together.

I watched the hospice nurse do her work. Everything seemed in order, and there was no job to keep me busy. I was overwhelmed by wonder. I was married now and the mother of three school-age children. I lived the stresses of family life, exhausted by the physical demands alone—organizing meals, driving carpools, balancing school schedules with my own. How did my mother do it? Where did she find the grit and the gumption? Even more astonishing, I realized now, how did she travel around the world with us, overcoming every barrier to access? I was there, at her side at every turn, and I still couldn't grasp the tenacity involved. My inability to comprehend her situation reminded me of my old dream about the blind boy. Those images—the extravagant party, the blind boy, the gilded frame—had never really left me. They were as vivid as when I dreamed them as a sixteen-year-old.

Now, though, I was drawn to a different aspect of the dream. That gold frame—the sturdy ornate border that encased the canvas and set it apart—took on new significance. The frame formed a boundary between what could be shared and what remained personal, incapable of transmission. I remembered the blank white canvas and my eyes welled up. My wonder tuned to sorrow. I was sorry for this mother and daughter. And for that teenage girl and the blind boy too. I ached somehow for the metal wheel and the gold frame that brought those pairs together and kept them apart. Yes, I pushed my mother's chair and tended to her needs, but I did not experience her paralysis. I was not with her in her darkest nights. Polio was hers alone.

3. June 2009

Mom died on June 10, 2009, just days after she encouraged the malekhamoves to remain in her living room, beating its wings. She let go gracefully at four o'clock in the morning, the darkest part of the night. Harry and I stood at her bedside. Her last breath was imperceptible from the one just before.

4. January 2022

But this story does not end with my mother's death. Mom's presence remains a powerful force. I imagine her responses as I grapple with new chapters of my life: letting go of adult children, aging with grace. And I still rethink old junctures in our relationship. How conflicted she must have been when she took me to Warm Springs. Why did she never visit my schools? Did she think I'd be embarrassed by her presence? You can see that our story continues.

This constant unfolding reminds me again of the blind boy in my high school dream. When I think about him now, I recognize that the blind boy is me. Yes! I have guided you down a path, pointing a direction, excited to share myself with you. I envision us traveling together as I offer you glimpses into a different kind of life. But I do not know what you will see in these pages. You weren't there. You didn't grow up in Dallas, tour the world in 1970 full of self-searching and devotion. I don't know how you will relate to my teenage travails.

So I am not going to stop here with a final period, as if this story has a neat finish. Let us remain together instead, shoulders together and arms entwined, journeying down this path we have begun. Go ahead. You take the next step. You try now. Tell me, if you are able, what is it that you see?

ACKNOWLEDGMENTS

This book began in Eden Elieff's Dallas living room with a group of curious and creative women who have remained among my dearest friends. I am so grateful to each of you for your careful reading and joyous enthusiasm: Eden Elieff, Nancy Allen, Jaina Sanga, Rita Juster, Julie Hersh Kosnik, Lauren Embrey, Kaleta Doolin, Donna Wilhelm, and Trea Yip. The book took shape while I studied for a certificate in creative nonfiction at Stanford University's continuing education program. I am especially thankful to Luanne Castle who pushed me: "No, tell me—*why* were you traveling to India in 1970 with your mother?" The answer to that question led to the narrative arc of this story. It is to Peter Kline at Stanford that I am most deeply indebted. Peter, my beloved teacher and guide, patient and persistent. Your belief in this story and my ability to tell it is the only reason this book is a reality. I stumble to find the right words to express my appreciation. The team at Deep Vellum has been sensational. Thank you, Will Evans, for saying over our first cup of coffee, "I'll publish your book!" And thank you, Jill Meyers, editor extraordinaire. Harry, thank you. Your memory of moments I had forgotten helped fill in the "separate trip we took together"! But my fullest gratitude begins and ends with my amazing husband, Stephen Lerer. You, Stephen, are the steady center of my world. Because of you, it takes on shape and substance. And thank you to our fabulous children, Joe, Lilly, and Katie, who keep our world constantly spinning.

PARTNERS

pixel ||| texel

EMBREY FAMILY
FOUNDATION

ADDITIONAL DONORS, CONT'D

Mark Haber
Mary Cline
Maynard Thomson
Michael Reklis
Mike Soto
Mokhtar Ramadan
Nikki & Dennis Gibson
Patrick Kukucka
Patrick Kutcher
Rev. Elizabeth & Neil Moseley
Richard Meyer

Scott & Katy Nimmons
Sherry Perry
Sydneyann Binion
Stephen Harding
Stephen Williamson
Susan Carp
Susan Ernst
Theater Jones
Tim Perttula
Tony Thomson

SUBSCRIBERS

Alan Glazer
Amber Williams
Angela Schlegel
Austin Dearborn
Carole Hailey
Caroline West
Courtney Sheedy
Damon Copeland
Dauphin Ewart
Donald Morrison
Elizabeth Simpson
Emily Beck
Erin Kubatzky
Hannah Good
Heath Dollar

Heustis Whiteside
Hillary Richards
Jane Gerhard
Jarratt Willis
Jennifer Owen
Jessica Sirs
John Andrew Margrave
John Mitchell
John Tenny
Joseph Rebella
Josh Rubenoff
Katarzyna Bartoszynska
Kenneth McClain
Kyle Trimmer
Matt Ammon

Matt Bucher
Matthew LaBarbera
Melanie Nicholls
Michael Binkley
Michael Lighty
Nancy Allen
Nancy Keaton
Nicole Yurcaba
Petra Hendrickson
Ryan Todd
Samuel Herrera
Scott Chiddister
Sian Valvis
Sonam Vashi
Tania Rodriguez

AVAILABLE NOW FROM DEEP VELLUM

FORTHCOMING FROM DEEP VELLUM